# WHY LIMIT WIP

## WE ARE DROWNING IN WORK

### A Modus Cooperandi MemeMachine

Modus Cooperandi Press

A Division of Modus Cooperandi, Inc.

1900 West Nickerson, Suite 116-88

Seattle, WA 98119

ISBN 978-0-989081-2-3-8

Modus Cooperandi MemeMachine Three

Why Limit WIP
We Are Drowning In Work
by Jim Benson

Version 1.1, 2014

Cover Photo "Balancing WIP" taken in Ho Chi Minh City, Vietnam
by Tonianne DeMaria Barry

LACK OF KNOWLEDGE...THAT IS THE PROBLEM.

~ W. EDWARDS DEMING

SUCCESS IN THE MARKETPLACE
INCREASINGLY DEPENDS ON LEARNING,
YET MOST PEOPLE DON'T KNOW HOW TO LEARN.

~ CHRIS ARGYRIS

# WIP = WORK IN PROGRESS
## WORK CURRENTLY BEING DONE

# TABLE OF CONTENTS

# WELCOME TO THE MEMEMACHINE

The purpose of the MemeMachine series is fourfold:

1. To introduce an emerging thought or a thought-in-process;

2. To explore that concept in practice;

3. To provide just enough material from each to give the non-specialist a basis for understanding and immediate implementation; and

4. To generate conversation and exploration of that idea within the larger community and help spawn communities of practice.

As the name "Modus Cooperandi" implies, collaboration is paramount to every endeavor we undertake and the cornerstone of our values. Rather than offer the "final say," we strive for community engagement in an effort to combine our shared experiences. Drawing from our collective insight we can develop, modify, validate, and refine an emerging idea and watch that meme evolve organically rather than dogmatically.

We chose to format this work as a MiniBook to quickly disseminate a distinct idea: *working beyond capacity negatively impacts individuals and teams.* The MiniBook format is simple in terms of structure: rather than overwhelm with every facet of a new concept—in this case, limiting work-in-progress (WIP)—the MiniBook format is intended to introduce a concept and start a conversation.

So let's have a conversation. If through the course of this MiniBook you find there are topics you'd like to discuss more in depth, we welcome you to reach out to us and others via social media. To connect with us on Twitter use @ourfounder, @sprezzatura, or @ModusCoop. To connect with and engage other members of this community of practice, use the hashtag #moduscoop. And of course, you can contact us online at moduscooperandi.com.

As always, we encourage your engagement and look forward to hearing from you.

Jim Benson
Tonianne DeMaria Barry
Modus Cooperandi
Seattle, WA

# PREFACE
## WE ARE DROWNING IN WORK

CHRIS HEFLEY
*CEO, LEANKIT*

As a business owner, I know that we *are* drowning in work.

Almost everything about the modern workplace allows for unlimited signals of incoming demand for our time, attention, and energy. As a result, we waste an incredible amount of our scarce resources on managing, re-prioritizing, and reporting on large amounts of in-process work. At any given time, we tend to have many, many things started, and it often feels like we're getting fewer and fewer things done.

Having too much work in process—and not getting enough of the important work done—applies as much to organizational leadership as it does to the team level and personal time management. An organization that can effectively limit its work in process, narrow its focus to the most important things, and then get those things deployed into the marketplace will have a competitive advantage. Started-but-not-finished things aren't delivering any benefit to the organization, be it revenue generation, cost savings, or market intelligence. A thing that is done and deployed into the market can be learned from, responded to, and maximize its revenue generation, innovation, and cost savings benefits.

Our success isn't measured in how many things we are working on. It only matters how much we actually get done.

This book, better than any other, lays out the case for limiting work in process. And it is through limiting work in process that we're actually able to get more things done.

But limiting work in process is hard. Very hard. We (humans) aren't wired for it. Our organization cultures aren't hospitable to it. It's certainly not the kind of thing that just happens naturally. You don't "self-organize" your way into limiting work in process.

It takes leadership.

Teams don't usually have the political capital, discipline, or authority to effectively limit their own work in process. And it (usually) takes more than giving them permission to limit their own WIP. In my experience, teams can only do this on a very limited basis, and only until the next urgent problem arises. It's up to the leaders of the organization to insist on limiting work in process and allow teams to focus on getting things done.

Limiting WIP forces you to face hard choices about your organization's capacity and the priority of work entering the system. Those hard choices were there all along, but just "getting started" on something allows you to feel good about it, without regard to the actual effect on your ability to get things done. It's much harder to say "we won't start that work until the fourth quarter" than it is to say "go ahead and get started, along with all the other things you're already doing." Never mind that starting a new project causes all of the work in process to take longer and delay its entry into the marketplace. At least we feel good about having gotten started on something.

I've been waiting for this book for a long time. It's a leadership fable, in the style of Patrick Lencioni or Eli Goldratt, that describes a fictional company and its fictional crisis as a way of illustrating the very real principles behind limiting work in process, getting things done, and the leadership required to make it happen.

At LeanKit, we so strongly believe in the principles of limiting WIP and the leadership required to do it effectively that we commissioned a special edition of this book for our staff and customers. I hope that you'll enjoy this book as much as we have, and I trust that it will serve you well in your journey towards limiting your WIP, just as it has helped us.

Chris Hefley
CEO, LeanKit

# FOREWORD
## IGNORE AT YOUR PERIL

GENE KIM
CO-AUTHOR *THE PHOENIX PROJECT*

*Personal Kanban* transformed how we think about our own personal productivity. *Why Limit WIP* will transform how organizations and teams think about and manage their work. The tale in this book will hurt, because you'll have undoubtedly lived with the consequences of people being stretched too thin, work constantly blocked or in queue, projects chronically late, and people getting burned out.

The symptomatology of what happens when organizations don't visualize their work and limit their WIP is brilliantly described. More importantly, the prescribed steps and countermeasures to enable fast flow of work is unassailable and based on common sense and a deep knowledge of the domain. Their recommendations are based on the work they've done implementing successful transformations in scores of organizations.

Implementing the measures in this book may require overcoming a lifetime of bad habits, but is a journey that I've personally committed myself to. I recognize my own dysfunctions in the problems they describe, and the importance of relentless striving to master these skills.

I'm certain that ten years from now, these techniques will become common practice in high performing organizations. Ignore these lessons at your peril.

Gene Kim

Co-author of *The Phoenix Project: A Novel About IT, DevOps, and Helping Your Business Win*

Founder and former CTO of Tripwire, Inc.

# INTRODUCTION
## THE ELDRED SAGA

▶ **Do not plan for ventures before finishing what's at hand. ~Euripides**

Even in Euripides' day 2400 years ago, people were plagued by starting new work before completing what they'd already begun. Today, relationships, projects, the media, and the Internet inundate us with options—with new and exciting things to begin. Workers become overloaded with tasks—both sanctioned and unsanctioned—that often provide little value to customers or the company. Their overload leaves them scrambling to get to meetings, to manage increasing overhead for each additional task, and to come up with excuses for delays.

We love to start things, but we're much less interested in finishing them.

This might be interpreted as procrastination, which can of course be a factor. But the real issue is that our work systems value the starting line more than the finish tape. We have many stakeholders asking where we are on their task; they want to know what we are starting for them—

they are much less interested in what we are currently completing for someone else.

Business is suffering a crisis of work-in-progress (WIP) at the expense of completion. We are doing too much work, yet we are producing too little product and by extension, too little value. Unfortunately, our response to this is often to start more projects.

Sometimes when I mention this to people they tell me how they usually make their deadlines. When asked if they make their deadlines in a low-stress environment, they *laugh*.

So while they do meet their deadlines, the product has been created under duress, bringing with it defects caused by pushing the work out at the last minute. These defects create future work which might be a report returned due to inaccuracies or typos, software with too many bugs, or a product returned at the store.

We think we are making our deadlines, but we are not actually completing our work. Overload is causing shoddy workmanship. We want to build products that don't get returned. Rework is not success.

▶ In a plant where required numbers actually dictate production, I like to point out that the slower but consistent tortoise causes less waste and is much more desirable than the speedy hare who races ahead and then stops occasionally to doze. The Toyota Production System can be realized only when all the workers become tortoises.
~ Taiichi Ohno, *Toyota Production System: Beyond Large-Scale Production*

*If we are starting too much and finishing too little,
wouldn't it make sense to start less and finish more?*

Throughout the last several years, my business partner Tonianne and I have been surprised by the Swiss Army knife that is limiting WIP. Limiting WIP is a simple, versatile tool, resulting in people examining their work, eliminating unnecessary tasks, and finishing valuable products faster. And that's only the beginning.

So, here's our conundrum. When we tell people:

*You can't do more work than you can handle.*

Everyone gets that.

Everyone seems to understand that when we are overcapacity...we are over capacity.

C-level execs, economists, bankers, nurses, middle managers, moms—everyone gets the truth in that statement. They nod. They acknowledge it is a problem. They agree that overloading people makes them ineffective.

But simply saying "You can't do more work than you can handle" doesn't compel people to act. There are too many confounding variables. There are no patterns of behavior to limit our WIP. Politics, commitments, and a fundamental lack of understanding of work from all angles make limiting work-in-progress seem unrealistic.

To put it bluntly: **It's no one's job to limit their WIP.**

We need to change that.

This MemeMachine is intended to provide some structure around why it is vital that we limit our work-in-progress and offer suggestions to achieve it. To these ends, this book tells two simultaneous tales:

- The effects of and treatments for overwork on the personal, team, and corporate level, and

- The roles of leadership, management, and production in a healthy modern business.

It all comes back to the sentence:

*You can't do more work than you can handle.*

But why? Why can't we do more work than we can handle? What happens when we exceed our WIP?

We live in a world that overloads us with information and expectations. We want to help others. We place ourselves in situations where saying "No" makes sense to no one—not even ourselves. We place others in positions where they need to complete things for us, when we have no understanding of what their workload is.

As bosses, we see people's time as finite and easily divisible. We believe our estimates and we believe that work only happens within the Gantt chart. We place our blind faith into plans. We delude ourselves, believing our future is neat and orderly with projects beginning and ending on schedule and value being delivered all as we foresee. There is a word for this: *clairvoyance.*

# WE ARE DROWNING IN WORK

Humans don't possess clairvoyance.

What we need is to understand that knowledge work is susceptible to a high degree of variation. Tasks that we think will take hours can take weeks. Indeed one repeated task can take widely varying amounts of time.

We need to *think* about our work. We need to build systems that focus on actually completing value and not merely starting projects. We need to make hard decisions.

Paradoxically to some, the less we start the more we finish—in both the short and long terms.

And that's what this MemeMachine is about.

We want to explore the problems of variation and overload. There are personal, organizational, and societal issues that must be dealt with in order for businesses and the people in them to thrive.

Let's take some time now and examine why limiting WIP is necessary, why it is a challenge, and why people so often give up trying to work within their capacity.

# CHAPTER 1
## PROCESSING & MEMORY

Business runs on brainpower. No matter what we make, the primary engine of wealth and value creation is the human mind. We have ideas and we translate those ideas into goods and services.

The brain is an idea engine, a creative engine, and a profit engine.

Like any other engine, we can overload it for a time and during that time it will produce more. But that time is brief and comes with costs. The engine must be maintained or it will burn out.

When we look at the speedometer on our car, we see on the far right side a very large number. If we drove that fast all the time, we could certainly arrive at our destination more quickly. However, we would crash often and ultimately destroy the car (and ourselves...and maybe a few bystanders as well).

This is exactly how we drive business today. We habitually take on too much work, destroying our ability to actually get work done. This is a systemic problem. It has managerial, personnel, and product impacts. In this book we'll cover all of those, but right now let's get to the heart of the (gray) matter: our brains.

## THE ZEIGARNIK EFFECT

In 1927, Soviet psychologist Bluma Zeigarnik noticed and described a certain phenomenon: when we finish tasks we get closure and move on. When we don't finish tasks…we don't. This was dubbed the "Zeigarnik Effect."

We keep thinking about those unfinished tasks. They haunt us. We yearn for completion.

Indeed, our unfinished tasks become constant small-scale thought disruptions. Everything we leave incomplete is therefore an interruption, robbing us of focus.

Zeigarnik was a student of the "Gestalt School" of psychology. Loosely translated as "whole" or "form" and with its focus on how cognitive processes are organized, Gestalt incorporates elements of philosophy and assumes a whole person, holistic approach. Deeming human thoughts, actions, and feelings as inseparable, it has influenced today's work in systems thinking and pattern languages.

Today, there is much research focusing on how human memory works and what happens when we disrupt it. In this MemeMachine, we could approach the impacts of the Zeigarnik Effect from many different angles: multitasking, context switching, interruptions, having too many projects, etc. Indeed later sections of this book will deal specifically with these issues.

For now, let's start with our individual memory processing. How do we actually think and remember?

We have a lot of different memory systems. These systems interact quite well most of the time. But, like any system, they can become overloaded. As we become overloaded with distractions and choices, our memory systems become fatigued and break down. That's not a good thing.

# HOW DOES THIS SYSTEM WORK

First, let's take a look at a few key memory system elements:

**Procedural Memory** is where we store the steps we take to do something. We learn this by rote and repetition. Do something a certain way, do it again, and again...*practice.* This type of memory gives our brains a break so we don't have to constantly re-invent our processes or drag them out of memory like we were trying to recall the name of the girl who sat next to us in the fourth grade.

**Short Term or Active Memory** is extremely short. Research on exactly how short is divided. Some measures of short term memory are as brief as eighteen seconds, while others treat short term memory as a decaying continuum stretching out up to ten minutes. What researchers seem to agree on is the fragility of short term memory. Short term memory is highly susceptible to interruption and distraction. Its short life-span makes it unreliable. We are quite good at remembering small details for short periods of time, but only if we maintain focus on them. As we overload or exceed our short term memory buffer, we have sharp decreases in memory fidelity.

**Working Memory** is where we manipulate things: figures, concepts, active elements of real-time work that may or may not be necessary in the future. If you are cooking a roast, you will store in active memory where you put the oregano and the bottle of red wine. Your memory of these locations is likely to last only as long as you need them, but will likely not be stored in long term memory. These are tactical or situational specific items. This is a high fidelity, short term system that is bolstered by a consistent context and with the general limit of seven to nine items. If our context involves several concurrent tasks or other distractions, that adds to the variables that working memory needs to store and can quickly overload it.

**Long Term Memory** is much longer, ranging from 10 minutes to forever. This is where we store information that our brain deems necessary to remember or simply has the time to retain. There is a complex system of interrelated brain features that govern what we remember. We tend to remember things that scare us more than we do things that bring us joy. We tend to remember exceptions rather than "normal stuff." We tend to remember things when we take time to let our brains relax and process.

We saturate our brains with things to remember. The brain can't keep up when we are slamming away at work, going for eight hours straight—non-stop with no breaks.

Then, just a few days later, we have no memory of what we did. That's because our short term memory was so overtaxed that it had no time to convert those daily actions to long term memory.

Instead, what we do remember are all those unmet commitments.

Bluma Zeigarnik would say that we are focusing on the incomplete tasks and we let the completed ones fade away, no longer relevant in our emergency-driven life. Our overloaded work-in-progress is robbing us of our memories.

This is not a good thing. We need to remember what we have done.

*But what can help us here?*

In general, our brain is aided by a few things in the memory department:

**Coherence** If you go see a movie, you'll generally remember the plot long after you've left the theatre. The movie took longer than ten minutes and generally had a lot of sensory input. It was a coherent, fairly linear event that your brain could easily process.

**Concentration** If you focus on a small set of tasks, you concentrate in both senses of the word. You focus attention and concentrate your options. In the short term, you limit options in order to achieve a state where you can direct attention to a specific task. Again, with a movie, you are concentrating our attention on that movie for a much longer time than ten minutes.

**Sequestering** Many people now use Netflix or other streaming services to view movies at home. I'm willing to bet that they remember less of the movies they watch at home because in a movie theatre, we are sequestered. We are confined to a room in which nothing but the movie happens. At home, we are bombarded with distractions that direct our attention away from the movie, making the movie less memorable.

## WHAT THIS MEANS AT WORK

At work, when we don't limit our work-in-progress we end up meeting none of these criteria. We are distracted, over stimulated, and interrupted. This destroys our ability to process information and remember what we've done. This is a major destroyer of value.

Engaging multiple projects at once and being subjected to random disturbances:

**Destroys Coherence** When we try to work, answer e-mail, and switch back and forth between demands, we no longer have coherence. It would be like if we switched back and forth between *The Princess Bride*, *The Godfather*, a World Cup game, and CNN at random intervals. We might have an inkling of what was going on, but we would never really have "enjoyed" any of them.

**Forget Concentration** Again, in the example above, how much do you think you could concentrate?

**Sequestering? Not so much.** With utter disregard for sequestering, we find ourselves overloaded with media and unable to focus.

Now, try this: grab a copy of a technical book. Turn on your television—good and loud. Choose five stations and have someone else, at random times, switch back and forth between them. Start reading the book while trying to ignore the TV. Not only will you not get very far in your reading, you will likely become highly agitated, further decreasing your ability to process and remember.

Without coherence, concentration, and sequestering, we remember with much less fidelity. Work is stressful. The information we process is limited. We act on less complete thoughts. If your team, your employees, or you are working so hard that there is no memory of the work you are completing—you are flushing value down the drain.

## LIMITING WIP AND SEQUESTERING

When we limit our work-in-progress, people can concentrate on the task at hand. True sequestering is difficult and often impractical. We are not advocating that you completely isolate yourself from the organization for weeks on end. There is another alternative: *tactical sequestering.*

Tactical sequestering allows us to set aside time to concentrate for small, focused effect. Some of our clients regularly employ the *Pomodoro Technique*® in which an individual or a team focuses for 25 minutes on a specific task or set of tasks, takes a five minute break, then repeats. During the 25 minute working session, they cannot be disturbed. It's a small enough time that people can come back to interrupt them later, but long enough to get significant work done. It is likewise long enough to gain coherence around the work being done—aiding memory and reducing transaction costs for context switching.

# CHAPTER 2
## COMPLETION

At every organization I have visited over the last three years, I've noticed a recurring problem: people are overextended to the point of absurdity and it is destroying them.

I like to play a game with teams called "count the bosses." People believe that they can work on five, eight, even sixteen projects at once. If you can count more than three bosses actively asking you for something, you are highly unlikely to be productive or effective.

The Zeigarnik Effect has a nasty side effect: when people take on too much work they go looking for more work. One team I worked with was seriously overloaded. All their official projects were *months* behind schedule. Yet, they regularly took on little 20 minute "favors" for other parts of the company. This represented thousands of hours of unsanctioned, undocumented work.

*Why? Why would any sane person do this?*

It was because they wanted to *complete something*. As professionals, they had to see some value being created somewhere—no matter how small. The 20 minute favor could be done and they could go home knowing that they had some positive impact. Otherwise, they had only their bogged-down projects to look forward to.

Despite this, middle-management frequently throws up their hands. With an exasperated cry they say, *"O! Verily, I am smited by internal politics' steely hand! Have pity on my wretched soul!"*

In short, middle managers feel that they cannot tell those above them that actually completing work is preferable to doing tons of unproductive work.

Few workers feel they have the freedom to say "No" to any assignment given to them by a superior. Since they have no way of demonstrating that they are overloaded or need to focus on someone else's priority, knowledge workers feel compelled to take on any work that comes their way.

Enthusiastically, they accept this additional work because they want to do a good job and they actually care.

This is because knowledge workers rarely actually understand their work. Neither do their bosses, nor do their boss' bosses.

We simply don't understand the cost of non-completion.

So let me state categorically: **Right now your company is wasting time, money, and potential by not completing important projects.**

And not a little. A lot of time, money, and potential.

Oddly enough, when a business completes things, it can use them. It can learn from them. It can make money from them. And, perhaps most importantly, it can move on to new projects that in turn can create more value.

## WHY DO WE NOT UNDERSTAND OUR WORK?

People seem to think they are able to predict the future. Our plans, in reality, are someone's best guess—or even wish—as to what should happen. They almost always run afoul of what actually happens. Plans are created without any appreciation of the role of work's natural variation.

This is a good point to bring up the Planning Fallacy, a well-documented cognitive bias that shows how people routinely underestimate the length of tasks. In the MemeMachine *Why Plans Fail*, we discuss how a large part of our inability to estimate is due to a fundamental lack of understanding about the role of variation in our work.

So, let's look quickly at how we tend to plan a project:

1. You approach me with a project and ask for a plan;
2. Based upon my years of experience, I list out all the tasks I think that plan will require;
3. We talk about that list;
4. You tell me what the budget and deadlines are;
5. I make that list fit into the budget and deadlines;
6. We argue until someone "*wins*"; and
7. *Voila!* We now have a "plan."

Do you notice anything about that plan? It's based on some pretty shaky foundations:

First, **No Basis in Reality**—we never asked how long tasks might really take, we merely asked for someone to give us a plausible number.

Second, **Faith in Experience**—we assume that the project manager can make these judgments alone. This is a faith-based approach, not a scientific one.

Third, **Predetermination**—we made the plan fit into a budget and/or deadline which were set before the plan was ever written.

Fourth, **Clairvoyance**—we assume that the project manager will be able to see into the future and know which of those tasks will go horribly wrong.

Fifth, **Politics**—there are extreme political pressures to conform to the budget and deadline.

Sixth, **Inflexibility**—there are nearly zero provisions for convenient changes to the plan.

Seventh, **Contractual Obligations**—there is no guarantee that personnel initially assigned will remain dedicated to the project. There is no guarantee that the project will remain relevant. There is no guarantee that the project features will remain unchanged. Yet the project manager will be held to the estimate and plan as if they were etched in stone.

Despite all this, the project manager must make this plan happen.

*And...this is a best case scenario.*

And right now you are likely fighting both the recognition that this is how things work and the urge to tell me that *you don't do it that way.*

## PLANS AND PEOPLE COLLIDE

Our plans assume that certain people will work a certain percentage of their time on a certain project. Enter our mythical man: his name is Eldred.

Eldred is a conscientious employee. Everyone loves him. He is the greatest worker ever.

Eldred is slated to work on Project A, which is managed by Glenn. Glenn has put into his plan that he needs 10% of Eldred's time.

So Eldred starts to work on Project A, but he has lots of time for other projects.

Eldred then gets pulled onto Project B, managed by Iggy. That will take 15% of his time. So, now he's up to 25%. He, and everyone else, is worried he'll be laid off at such low utilization, so they put him to work helping with the very large Project C, managed by Crazy Larry. Crazy Larry says he'll take 30% of his time.

Eldred's now at 55%, which still isn't enough, so Lucy's Project D and Armin's Project E can both account for another 10% each. Now he's at a comfortable 75% utilization. Everyone agrees that's acceptable and to leave well enough alone.

All of a sudden, Eldred is very busy. While he's staying late at work, he's not actually completing anything. And people are getting annoyed. He's only at 75% utilization. What's his problem? Some people are doing just fine at a full 100% utilization on one or two projects.

With a comfortable 25% buffer, why has Eldred's performance suffered?

## WHAT DON'T WE UNDERSTAND?

Now this sounds like a great place to talk about the penalties of context switching. And indeed it would be, but we'll get to that a little later. Right now we need to cover something even more basic—the actual context of our work.

We feel, after years of project plans, Gantt charts, and professional experience that we can adequately foresee the future.

When we look through those seven issues with our plan, we find a long list of mitigatable, albeit unavoidable issues. The project will more than likely take longer than we anticipate. Elements of the project will change. There will be surprises in task duration, there will be unforeseen difficulties. There will be time-consuming contractual change orders.

When we select a task, we don't know how complex it will actually be. We are often surprised when tasks blow up in our faces. To make matters worse, we have limited ways to detect or communicate when we've suddenly found ourselves blindsided by a complex task.

If we limit our work-in-progress and focus on one project at a time—giving our work a sense of coherence—we may have more insight into problems as they occur. But if we are on two, three, or four projects, we sacrifice coherence and are unlikely to even spot problems until it is too late or mitigation too costly.

We spin more and more cycles trying to complete tasks on which we haven't time to focus.

So, if I have a task that takes 20 hours to complete and it's interrupted by other projects and expectations, it may have only taken me 20 hours (one half a work-week), but those 20 hours are spread out over months. By the time I am done with the task, I have no idea how long it really took and the cost of delay can be massive. What should have taken 2.5 days to deliver now took 2 months![1]

The real pain points for traditionally managed projects stem from running people and teams over their capacity. When I built large transportation projects like light rail systems, my team and I all worked on two to ten projects

---

[1]    I know that now you are saying "Why? Why?" and that's a good question. One with many answers. So sit tight and this question will be answered again, again, and again.

at once. We were all in Eldred's shoes. To make matters worse, we all had areas of expertise that resulted in everyone being sought out for short consultations on projects we weren't even assigned to. This combination of project and non-project overload meant that we were constantly stressed and late on deliverables.

Back when I was a consulting engineer, I was home working when at a little past midnight my colleague Claudia sent me an email asking for help. I immediately did what she needed and replied that it was done.

*What are you doing up working this late?* she asked, even though she was obviously working late as well.

*Sleep is for wimps!* I replied, wearing my overtime like a badge of honor.

Later I realized, sleep wasn't for wimps. Overwork was for simps and we were over-worked. The concept of an eight hour work day was unknown to anyone at my company.

## WE PLAN FOR THE IDEAL

We tend to plan our work assuming it will flow logically, with no screw ups, with no interruptions, with nothing unforeseen, and in an ideal amount of time.

So when one of our allegedly simple tasks suddenly gets complex (complex tasks are difficult to explain, and contain novel problems we didn't foresee), we don't have time for them. We then switch to something else, assuming we'll come back to that confusing task later. Complex tasks get buried under the pile of other work we are doing.

I have seen many long-delayed projects derailed by two or three unforeseen complex tasks. These tasks would have been expediently dispatched with simple WIP limits because people would have been forced to deal with them immediately.

Why? *Because limiting WIP enforces completion.*

## LIMITING WIP AND COMPLETION

Faced with all these competing demands, Eldred finds himself unable to complete any of his work in a timely fashion. One night after everyone has gone home, he realizes he's not even sure what he's working on any more. There's so much going on at the same time. Fed up, Eldred creates a Personal Kanban.

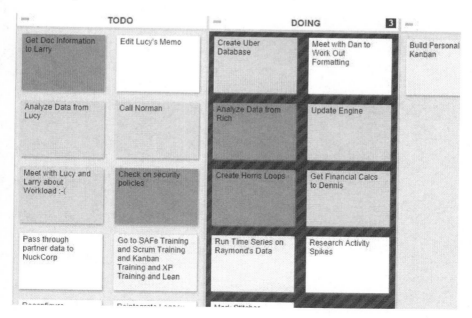

His DOING column immediately fills up with nine items—that's his personal WIP. He knows it's too much.

He shakes his head, beginning to realize what he's signed up for. "I've got way too much on my plate," he says to the empty office.

So Eldred works with his board a bit, does some prioritization, and comes up with something a little more reasonable. His updated Personal Kanban looks something like this:

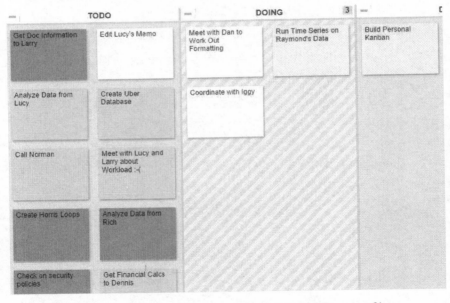

Eldred decides that he's going to limit his WIP even if he has to do it alone. This starts to help. But, he has work on several different projects. He's limited his WIP—but he is leaving some projects unattended. Eldred prioritized Iggy's project in the short term to get one particular deliverable out. Iggy is happy.

After a few days, Eldred's board looks like this:

| ODO | — | DOING | 3 | — | DONE |
|---|---|---|---|---|---|
| Analyze Data from Lucy | Run Time Series on Raymond's Data | Edit Lucy's Memo | | Build Personal Kanban | Mark Stitcher |
| Call Norman | Create Horris Loops | | | Meet with Dan to Work Out Formatting | Coordinate with I... |
| Analyze Data from Rich | | | | | |
| Get Financial Calcs to Dennis | | | | | |

Eldred is feeling pretty good. He can actually see what he is completing. We can see that he's been able to get a bunch of little tasks done. But the large task, working with Raymond's data, is stuck in **DOING.**

Despite feeling pretty good about all he is accomplishing, Eldred has a nagging feeling that he's not actually completing enough. Three days' work and all he was able to complete is four tickets? The kanban is now alerting Eldred that, while he may be busy, he's neither being *productive* nor *effective.* He is seeing the delta between what he believes to be reasonable progress and actual progress.

Once he sees this, he wants to complete more. "I am tired of being *busy,*" he thinks, "I want to *finish stuff.*"

He wants to get tickets to **DONE.**

# CHAPTER 3
## ON MULTITASKING & BOTTLENECKS

Eldred is in a bind. Even with his unilateral WIP limiting, he's still really working on all those projects at the same time. "It's okay," he thinks, "I have the three things I'm focusing on, but I'm a good multitasker. I can handle the interruptions as long as I know what I need to get done."

*Sigh.*

A 2009 Stanford study suggests that multitaskers…make really lousy multitaskers.[1]

*Whaaaa?*

Researchers found that self-identified multitaskers ended up being people who were merely justifying a scattered lifestyle. Perhaps they *felt* productive because during a day they touched so many different tasks, but when actually tested against people who focused on one thing at a time, the multitaskers failed…and failed big.

---

1    See: http://news.stanford.edu/news/2009/august24/multitask-research-study-082409.html

Why was this? Well, it was the Zeigarnik Effect writ large.

Here's what they did. The researchers put the "multitaskers" and the "unitaskers" in front of computers and asked them to complete a task. Then they would interrupt them and say, "No, do this other task." The information for both tasks remained visible on their screen. The goal was to focus on just a specific task in a specific location of the screen.

A Stanford News article described the results like this:

*They couldn't help thinking about the task they weren't doing,"* Eval Ophir said. *"The high multitaskers are always drawing from all the information in front of them. They can't keep things separate in their minds."*

*The researchers are still studying whether chronic media multitaskers are born with an inability to concentrate or are damaging their cognitive control by willingly taking in so much at once. But they're convinced the minds of multitaskers are not working as well as they could.*

*When they're in situations where there are multiple sources of information coming from the external world or emerging out of memory, [multitaskers are] not able to filter out what's not relevant to their current goal,"* said Anthony Wagner, an associate professor of psychology at Stanford. *"That failure to filter means they're slowed down by that irrelevant information.*

Now, what does this mean for Eldred?

# THE RIGHT ENVIRONMENT FOR SUCCESS

Our environment directly impacts our ability to think. Just like our movie example, when we are overstimulated, bombarded by distractions, we lose focus on our intended goal and direct our focus instead on the transitions between now competing goals and other distractions.

We are constantly in a state of processing change rather than processing value. That's an expensive transaction that we'll cover in the context-switching section coming up.

For now, let's talk about a high multitasking environment and what that looks like socially.

To illustrate, here's Eldred's official utilization:

Project A—10% time—Project Manager: Glenn

Project B—15% time—Project Manager: Iggy

Project C—30% time—Project Manager: Crazy Larry

Project D—10% time—Project Manager: Lucy

Project E—10% time—Project Manager: Armin

With 25% slack time, Eldred should be on Easy Street. If only Glenn, Iggy, Crazy Larry, Lucy, and Armin all lined up and just needed things from Eldred in succession. With each project having discrete demands, we can bet that Eldred is spending a lot of time managing those demands in meetings. We can further bet that some of the meetings are unproductive status updates so people can know where Eldred is at in his work.

While Eldred is actually working, each of his colleagues on the five respective projects are essentially a tactical nuclear missile aimed directly at Eldred's productivity. In one project, where there is a team of ten people, there is a certain percentage of Eldred's time that is spent talking to team members, coordinating, and just answering questions. Now, Eldred has five times the team members, five times the bosses, five times the products, and five times the customers.

Now I'm not going too far out on a limb by saying our time on Earth is finite. Eldred only has so many hours in the day. Even if he limits his WIP on his Personal Kanban, with five projects he's not minimizing interruptions. His projects create ambient work—they create ambient WIP. Eldred cannot escape the realities of the system in which he works.

These interruptions and meetings are not neatly scheduled. Eldred will be fielding questions from Projects A and C simultaneously. Crazy Larry will pull rank from time to time, saying that Eldred's not giving his full 30%. The other project managers will feel like Crazy Larry's project is getting attention at their expense. This will require more meetings to figure out Eldred's "resource utilization."

In the end, the company will have to hire contractors or temp workers to fill the apparent short staffing needs. Yet, since Eldred is now the go-to guy with vital information for all five projects **he must remain on all five projects.** Eldred will struggle to bring people up to speed and his interruptions will increase. The tickets on his Personal Kanban will move more and more slowly.

This is an extension of what Frederick Brooks wrote in *The Mythical Man Month.*[2] In essence, the greater the complexity a project's social structure, the slower the project will move. In this case, Eldred is a vital information source to his projects. He is sought out and has an even higher level of burden than normal. By placing Eldred in this situation, the managers have created a system that makes Eldred a bottleneck: all progress on the project slows to the rate at which Eldred can personally respond to interruptions.

## TASTES LIKE ELDRED-BERRY WINE

Eldred is not only overburdened, Eldred is a bottleneck. Over-stretching Eldred resulted in the slowdown of all five projects. Hiring more people to help out puts more pressure on the bottleneck without addressing the root cause. When this happens, Eldred has to interact with even more people.

When Eldred is overburdened, he slows down. As a result, his teams also slow down. The overall time it takes to finish work increases. The project slows down. Value production comes to a halt. Frustration abounds.

When we multitask, we increase the burden on our pro

Frederick Brooks, *The Mythical Man Month*, (Boston, Addison-Wesley, 1975).

cessing system—*our brains*. When we increase that burden, we decrease the throughput—the amount of work we can do at any given point in time. This reduces our personal throughput, which in turn impacts everyone around us. Our slower processing slows the entire system down.

In manufacturing there is a concept known as "takt time," the minutes of work necessary to complete a unit of value. The fastest takt time for a production line is as fast as its slowest station (it's not uncommon for the slowest time to be a bottleneck).

Let's be clear, the goal is not necessarily to get teams to work as fast as possible, but to remove the frustrations from our work that hinder us and shift our focus to how hard it is to finish things. We want to focus on finishing things, not on how difficult our lives are at work.

## SOLVING ELDRED'S DILEMMA

This particular issue is easily solved. Take Eldred off at least two of those projects.

Does that have impacts on the rest of the company? Yes!

Does that mean Eldred may have more slack time than we'd like? Does that mean Eldred gets to be lazy? Perhaps, but I doubt it. More likely it means that Eldred will be able to focus on the remaining projects which will still take up most or all of his time.

Questions about Eldred's utilization are normal...but they are the wrong questions.

A more productive question might be, "What do we want from Eldred and the company?"

### Do we want to actually finish and release things?

or

### Do we want to look busy?

I can tell you categorically, that there was no clear answer to this when I was a consulting engineer. When people hired us, they wanted us to look busy. If we didn't work on their projects for a few weeks, our clients would become angry, even if our hiatus meant that next week we'd come back and focus solely on their project. Even if that meant we were using our time effectively in the service of all of our projects. They wanted to see "progress," which didn't really mean progress...it meant "appearing active."

If we'd like to get a quality product out of Eldred quickly, we want to lower his project burden so he can focus on at most three projects (and preferably one).

When this happens, timeliness will *appear* to be impacted. But the overall completion rate of the company will radically increase. Yes, projects that are not being worked on will languish. But projects that are being worked on will be completed faster.

In the end, projects will be completed quicker, with higher quality, and less overhead.

# CHAPTER 4
# CONTEXT SWITCHING

Context switching is the Red Menace of modern day knowledge work.

Management theorist extraordinaire Jerry Weinberg has the go-to graph for context switching. Jerry shows that for every new project we take on our focus is immediately degraded.[1]

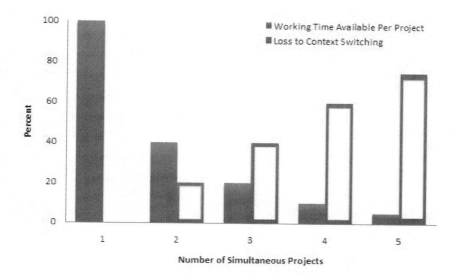

1     G.M. Weinberg, *Quality Software Management: Vol. 1 System Thinking. (New York. Dorset House, 1992).*

If we consider Eldred's five projects and Weinberg's graph, Eldred is doomed before he starts.

Jerry's chart shows us why limiting WIP is vital. When we context-switch, we lose time and fidelity. We incur costs in delay, overhead, and focus. We may think we seamlessly move from one project to another, but we don't.

Here's a quick exercise to show you the cognitive penalties for you, personally.

## Round One

Draw three columns. Start your timer. In the first column on the left write the letter "A", in the second column write the number "1", and in the third column write the Roman numeral "I".

Your first entry should look like this:

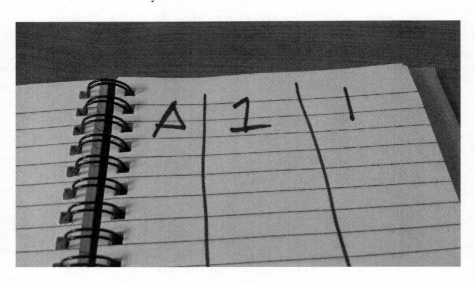

Now repeat that process, from left to right, populating each column *horizontally* with the next letter (B), number (2), and Roman numeral (II).

Your second entry should look like this:

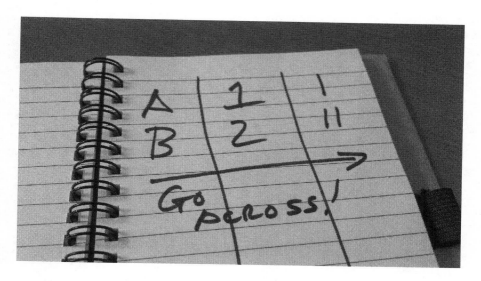

Do this through the letter J (J, 10, X).

When you are done, stop your timer and document your time.

## Round Two

Set your timer and repeat the exercise, but this time write the letters, numbers, and Roman numerals in sequence in each column *vertically* (A,B,C...1,2,3...I, II, III...).

Round two's entries should flow like this:

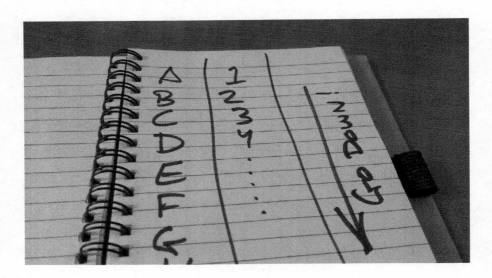

Again, continue to do this through the letter J (H, I, J...8,9,10...VIII, IX, X).

When you are done, stop your timer and document your time.

## THE PENALTIES OF CONTEXT SWITCHING

In the exercise above, I would be willing to bet your productivity was about 100% higher in the second exercise. Compared to the first exercise where you moved back and forth between systems, you were focused on one type of work at a time.

With an exercise this simple, where we only have three familiar variables to deal with, the penalties for context switching in a more complex environment are obvious.

We are now beginning to see that Eldred is not failing due to laziness or any direct action on his part, but rather, Eldred's failure is *systemic.*

Eldred's situation is violates some basic elements of human and social design. Every time he has to switch contexts, he is running up against cognitive limitations that decrease his ability to produce quality work.

As this dynamic unfolds, the individuals that comprise each team are becoming increasingly dissatisfied with the process, the products, and the company. Because Eldred is the primary visible bottleneck, they view him as the problem. They spending their time on countermeasures to deal with Eldred, when Eldred was never the problem in the first place.

In turn, the company is hemorrhaging money misguidedly keeping its people over-worked and under-focused. Eldred's company, in a quest for 100% utilization, is breaking the very equipment—their people—they are trying to optimize.

# CHAPTER 5
## CREATING AN ECONOMY

▶ **It's the economy, stupid.** ~ James Carville

You, right now, are disrespecting your ability to create amazing things.

You, right now, are trying to do more than you should, for more people than is optimal, and in an environment that is far too distracting.

Well, odds are you are doing those things.

*Why?*

Because right now, odds are overwhelmingly that you have no idea the full extent of the tasks you've assumed responsibility for, which ones you've subsequently left incomplete, and the costs for overextending yourself.

Odds are also (overwhelmingly) that you're a pretty decent person. You want to help people, you want to do a good job, and you are compelled to do interesting things.

And so, you repeatedly agree to take on new exciting things. Since there are no apparent penalties for saying "No," and seemingly obvious benefits to saying "Yes," why wouldn't you?

Why would we ever say "No" to helpful, interesting work? Especially when it's just one more task? It will only take five or ten minutes. It's just a little bit more work. And it's soooooooooo delicious...

Just as that one little Hershey's Kiss won't kill our diet, we justify one more task surely won't overload us.

The problem is, we're doing just one Kiss worth of work every hour...and they add up.

In our bathroom we have a scale that shows us the impact of those chocolates. Ideally we have a diet which regulates the flow of those chocolates. We built a system (the diet), with an economy (calories per day), that shows that there is an exchange rate between eating chocolate and gaining weight. We still want to eat chocolate, but we want to understand our eating economy. There is an exchange, with taxes and penalties, for over-indulging.

We've never really had an economic view of our work. We've never really paid attention to the relationship between overburdening and underdelivering. We've never really understood the exchange rate between the number of tasks in progress and product delivery. We've never really understood the opportunity costs of choosing one task over another.

Now we can.

Explicitly limiting work-in-progress creates that economy for our work. It shows us that there are direct penalties we pay for taking on too much. We can observe that our cognitive system degrades faster than our productivity improves. We can see that the more work we take on, the less we complete. We can understand that the work we choose at any point-in-time is a commitment to creating specific value that can only be realized when it is actually delivered to and accepted by our customers.

**Half-done work has little or no value.**

**Half-done work can rarely be sold.**

## IGNORING AN ECONOMY

In the global economic sense, we have seen that it is easy to overheat an economy and have it burn out with terrific penalties. We can see this in our daily lives. When there is no visible or obvious penalty to over use a resource, we tend to over use the resource. In this case, the resource is our own time.

Like bundling bad B & C loans into tradable packages, we gather up promises and shuffle them around. Each promise initially buys us good favor, until their debt load becomes so great that our economy collapses around us.

We live in a world of phony promise derivatives because we fundamentally don't understand the real value of the promises we make.

In our personal lives and in knowledge work, we see regularly that we take on too much, we get bogged down, everything becomes an emergency or a missed opportunity. Our world of promise derivatives becomes a world of panic trading and short-selling. We are rushing back and forth gathering as many late and increasingly value-less promises and finishing them as quickly as we can. Meanwhile, we are making new, fresh promises simply to keep the customer happy, even though we're terrified we won't deliver on those, either.

Panic generally does not result in meaningful product. Panic takes up mental capacity and time. Panic is overhead. Panic is now added to the overhead of managing over-work. After a while, panic feels like the order of things, which is unfulfilling personally and professionally.[1]

We need to avoid panic and its costly friends: waste, defects, and attrition.

## TWO MORE METAPHORS

Whether we are individuals, teams, or companies, we want to act on opportunities available to us. We make promises to others to realize these opportunities. Now, if these promises all took up physical space, they'd each come in a box, and we'd store them in our To-Do room.

---

[1]     Even more insidious is that as panic feels like the norm, a cognitive bias known as Status Quo Bias will arise. People will actually fight to maintain a panic-state in the organization, claiming it is motivating, warranted by the situation, or otherwise desirable.

After a while the room would fill up with promise boxes. "I can't fit more promise boxes." We'd say, "Come back later and I'll see if I have room then."

Well, bad news for us. Promises are not like boxes. Promises are like carbon monoxide. Promises are invisible, odorless, gaseous, and when they mount to dense enough concentrations they surprise us and kill us.

## BUILDING AN ECONOMY

Economies work better when they have minimal, but responsibly defined constraints.

Think of it this way: when Eldred's time was treated as a limitless resource he was quickly overutilized. Clock-based utilization of Eldred's time simply didn't work.

Two things became obvious:

1. He could not be optimized at 100% capacity or even 75%.

2. Different projects came with different cognitive overhead.

Eldred's time is more valuable than we thought. Initially, it seemed optimizing Eldred's time (utilization) was paramount. Now we see that Eldred's ability to produce requires sensitivity to how he processes information. We need to optimize for the most effective use of Eldred's brain.

Now we begin to have some building blocks for an economy.

We understand that Eldred is an awesome knowledge worker and can produce a great stuff, as long as Eldred and those around him understand his work.

Our work economy has the following elements:

1.  **Market Requirements** Eldred interacts with his products, his co-workers, his bosses, and his clients. These very necessary interactions have rules, needs, and transaction costs.

2.  **Variation in Currency** Eldred's work is knowledge work. Some days things go as planned. Some days things require him to put his head down and focus or gather his co-workers and really pound on a sticky problem. Often these states change without notice.

3.  **Adaptive Market Behavior** Eldred constantly needs to take in information, learn new things, process changes in context, and discuss this information with others. This means he needs to be able to focus, build coherence in his work, deal with change, and work through completion.

4.  **Market Health** Eldred is human. He gets weary. He interacts with other humans within and beyond his team. The interactions, information, and changes in context he is experiencing impact his and others' mood, psychological state, and ability to perform.

When our economy takes these things into consideration, we can begin to alter our working systems to support these parameters.

## LIMITING WIP IN THE NEW ECONOMY

While there are many other elements to managing this economy, limiting work-in-progress is right at the forefront.

In this new economy, work-in-progress is a primary currency. We now understand that limiting WIP provides time to concentrate, creates work coherence, and allows us to actually deliver. Just like the US Federal Reserve can adjust interest rates to regulate the economy, we use WIP limits to regulate the flow of work.

What we are surprised to learn is that doing fewer things simultaneously means we complete more things. We optimize for throughput and quality, as opposed to utilization and politics. Managing our economy means we are able to release more while doing less, simply because we are spending more time working and less time context-switching, politicking, status updating, and reacting to delay.

# CHAPTER 6
# HEALTHY CONSTRAINTS

▶ **Great floods have flown from simple sources. ~William Shakespeare**

In the previous section, we defined our work's economy. This economy needs healthy constraints. When you think about it, a system—*any system*—is simply a set of rules designed to achieve a goal or set of goals. Any healthy system needs just enough rules (constraints) to promote the desired outcome. Any more and it becomes mired down.

When we employ healthy constraints, we encourage flow within the system. In our work economy, our goal is to create a flow of work that results in a flow of value creation that in turn results in a flow of revenue that enables us to keep up with the flow of work. In other words, we want some degree of sustainability.

When it comes to constraints, we can either operate with healthy constraints, no constraints whatsoever, or too many constraints. Let's look at water to simplify

## HEALTHY CONSTRAINTS—FLOW

With a river, the right constraints promote healthy flow. Banks channel the water, dams restrict waterflow to an acceptable rate, and levies keep the water moving in the right direction. In the picture on the left, we have a garden on the shore, as commercial boats travel up and down the waterway.[1] In this controlled environment, we enjoy predictability and the ability to act.

In this case, the healthy constraints on the river give us the first picture. Water is tamed and the couple is enjoying the view. Healthy constraints provide value.

---

1    *Flood image courtesy of Melissa Will.*

# ZERO OR FAILED CONSTRAINTS—FLOODING

In our second picture, the river does not adhere to the constraints. The result is destructive flooding. Something in the system has broken down. A constraint has either failed (a dam breach) or there were insufficient constraints (the property should have had a floodwall to guard against the flood).

With insufficient constraints, value is ruined. Rather than spending time in the garden and enjoying the nice view, we spend our time reacting to the flood waters. We are now working to avoid or repair destruction rather than create value.

In this case, a lack of constraints caused by too much WIP (water-in-progress?) caused destructive flooding which not only drove the couple inside, but also utterly destroyed their beautiful garden.

# TOO MANY CONSTRAINTS—DIMINISHED FLOW

The other extreme (not pictured) would be a huge dam upstream from the property which would remove all water from the river. This would leave a big muddy mess, no commercial boat traffic, and no view for the couple to enjoy. This type of over-regulation dries up value, not allowing any system at all for it to flourish. It's popular to blame this behavior on government, but it seems to be a universal human condition—companies seem to commonly set up restrictive systems that undermine internal innovation and value creation.

# A STORY ABOUT FLOW

At my software company, Gray Hill Solutions, we had a project that dealt with precisely this issue. The US Forest Service manages a 4.3 million acre forest in east-central Idaho called the Salmon-Challis. The Salmon River and its tributaries run through this forest on its way to the Columbia. There are many private landowners that have property either adjacent to or spanning the river. These landowners often use some of the water from the river.

When landowners take water from the river, it is technically called a "diversion." We can call it a constraint.

One day some environmental groups filed a complaint with the US Forest Service because there were so many diversions that the Salmon River could no longer support the spawning of salmon. This is called "water-starvation" and was leading to low levels not only in the Salmon River but also arguably the Columbia. This was a problem for ecological and economic reasons. Salmon habitat was being destroyed and salmon fishing is a $603 billion dollar industry in Alaska alone (and many of those Alaskan catches are spawned in Idaho, Washington and Oregon).[2]

There were so many constraints in the system that water (and the salmon) would not flow.

One type of value in the Salmon-Challis economy was forsaking another. There was no balance.

---

2    See http://www.eenews.net/public/climatewire/2012/07/18/1

In order to make those constraints (and by extension, the river) healthy, the USFS needed to catalog all the diversions and see which were actually sanctioned. Then it had to mitigate the non-sanctioned diversions and restore the river to health. In other words, it needed to map out and understand its work, then figure out the right WIP limits (or DIP limits—diversions-in-progress?) to put into place.

## BALANCE AND HEALTHY CONSTRAINTS

When we limit our work-in-progress, we are seeking to place balanced, healthy constraints onto our work economy that promote healthy flow.

**Too Much** If we limit our WIP too much, we will be single-mindedly working on one task at a time and ignoring all else—with large potential social costs. We will dry up our ability to converse and collaborate. We will over-focus.

**Not Enough** No WIP limiting creates the flood of work we see every day. People overloaded. High costs of delay. Poor quality.

**Balance** You know, there's a reason that they call it a "balancing act." The world spins on its axis as it hurtles through space. Our continents are all inexorably continuing their drifting ways. Tectonic plates cause tremors in the most stable of locations. Change is constant. Disruptions are the norm. Balance, forever and without fail, is impossible.

Understanding what it is we are balancing—that's vital.

# WHAT MAKES A HEALTHY CONSTRAINT

▶ **If you're interested in 'balancing' work and pleasure, stop trying to balance them. Instead make your work more pleasurable. ~ Donald Trump**

Yes, that's right. Even Donald Trump gets it.

When we seek balance, too many rules (constraints) can be self-defeating. Each rule that we add is another brick in the dam of our river. Yes, it can control the flow—but it's a brick. Once it's cemented into place, you can only remove it with force (like dynamite) and the removal is not without its own impacts.

So, as The Donald is suggesting, sometimes the creation of a healthy constraint is based on your current point of view (which should and does change over time). Often limiting work-in-progress does not require us to make new rules, but to simply accept that overloading ourselves and our systems is counter-productive.

We can have rules and we can have realizations. We can have process and we can have principles. The former are hard constraints, the latter are much softer.

Simply setting a WIP limit on our Personal Kanban is a visual indicator of our commitment to this minimal constraint.

Pictured here is Derek Huether's Personal Kanban[3]. Derek is currently sticking to his WIP limit. There are a few tasks which are blocked, but by and large work looks like it is flowing well. It's flowing well today.

Tomorrow might be a different story. Derek's dishwasher could explode or his cat could destroy a piece of furniture or his tire might blow out or any number of things. Hopefully these won't happen, but if they did and he had to pull a fourth emergency item into his WIP column—he has the capacity to do so.

Derek has taken no blood-oath saying he will never exceed his WIP limit. This is a *healthy constraint*—not a law.

This flexibility gives Derek the freedom and autonomy to deal with situations as they arise. The fourth work item in

*Personal Kanban image courtesy of Derek Huether, http://thecriticalpath.info/*

WIP will not make him pay a fine or cost him his job, but it will make him aware that he is violating the constraint and that there will be penalties in completion time and quality of the items currently in-flight.

The healthy constraint in the kanban reminds Derek of what healthy work looks like.

If some emergency comes along and forces him into the realm of four, he will understand why he is overloaded and work to get back to his regular WIP limit of three.

To drive this point home, let's quickly define healthy and unhealthy constraints.

**Healthy Constraint** The minimum constraint required to reward a desired behavior while retaining maximum flexibility.

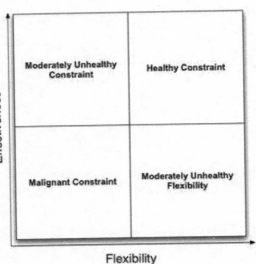

**Moderately Unhealthy Constraint** Codifies and makes mandatory desired behavior, but limits flexibility.

**Moderately Unhealthy Flexibility** Provides a great deal of flexibility but no guidance or expectations.

# CHAPTER 7
# FOCUS

▶ **You can't depend on your eyes when your imagination is out of focus.**
**~Mark Twain**

"Hey El, how was your weekend?"

"Good, Gerry, relaxing. I went hiking with friends up to Pollard Lake. How was yours?"

"Yeah, hey, I'd like you to get rolling on that memo we talked about. The faster I get it, the faster I can get moving."

Eldred comes into work on Monday morning looking forward to the week. His enthusiasm is soon replaced by stress. He is immediately besieged by competing requests for information, work, meetings, and product from all five of his teams. His co-workers, his bosses, his clients all need things from him, and they need them now.

Requests from all his projects are coming in so fast that he is having a hard time remembering them all. He has no time to prioritize or even judge the relative importance of these requests. It's possible that they are all equally valuable, but who knows? There is no clear direction for him to take.

His to-do list is on his whiteboard. Soon it's hard to read with sloppy erasing, insertions of new tasks, and side notes serving as futile attempts to prioritize. Each time he begins a task, someone asks where he is on another. Forget context switching, Eldred can't even choose a context to begin with!

Exasperated, Eldred finally calls his five bosses together and cries out, *"Just tell me what to do!"*

## ELDRED'S GOT NO FOCUS

Knowledge work happens within our brains. It is a product of the mind. Without imagination, without insight, without inspiration, it is simply *work.*

Knowledge work is not simply "work"—it is value creation by invention. Value creation includes the word "creation" for a reason. It's not value reproduction. Or value step-following. Knowledge workers solve unforseen problems. They create. They innovate.

Innovation requires focus. When we lose our ability to focus, we greatly impair our ability to get creative work done. We become reactive. We wait for people to sanction our actions. We lose the ability to describe our work. We stop looking for ways to help. Competing stakeholders vie for attention and resources, providing no clear direction and creating confusion as to what is really best for the company.

To cope with this confusion we begin to demand our bosses, *"Tell us what to do!"*

What's worse, we believe *that's what we want.*

A few words of advice:

**As a boss,** if your employees or team members are asking that question – you know they have no focus.

**As a boss,** if you insist on telling your staff what to do—*you're wasting your money paying knowledge workers to implement rather than invent.* You are creating a brittle enterprise.

## LEARNED HELPLESSNESS

When a person specifically asks someone else to tell them what to do, one thing is quite clear:

### THEY DON'T KNOW WHAT TO DO

Managers of knowledge workers, I have bad news for you.

This is your fault, and you need to fix it.

Eldred's bosses all start to argue. They all have the highest need for Eldred right now. Their projects are running behind and they, personally, cannot abide any more delays. As individuals, each manager is invested in their own interests, this means they are not invested in the company's interests.

Eldred sits and watches as his bosses argue. He feels responsible for this. If he'd only worked a little faster or put in a couple of extra nights this would have been avoided.

Eldred also feels...something else.  He feels...*annoyed*. He feels like he's wasting his time and thinks his leaders are all ineffectual middle management suck-ups. He feels like maybe he would be better served quitting right now and walking out the door and going to work somewhere else.

*Which he'd do if he weren't so ineffective and had to have managers argue to fix his mistakes.*

Now Eldred is thinking about his five projects, his own effectiveness, his managers, his career, his shame, and... you get the idea. The environment of project distraction has created additional personal and political distractions.

Not only does this dynamic create unnecessary meetings of people arguing about Eldred's time, also creates some-thing psychologists call "learned helplessness."

Learned helplessness results from situations in which we feel we are utterly powerless to act.

An example of this for me comes from the 7th grade. I had an algebra teacher who was a tyrant. After I had the flu, I sat for an exam that I utterly bombed. When I repeatedly went to him for help, he told me I should study harder. When I said that I had been sick, he told me that wasn't his problem. I had nowhere to turn and my shame made me not approach my peers. Whenever I talked to the teacher, he let me know this was my problem. Other students got sick and were doing just fine. My lack of understanding of things at the beginning of the class led to me falling farther and farther behind. Ultimately I failed the class, believing it was all due to my inability to learn algebra.

I was convinced this was my substandard brain in action.

My parents were concerned, but also were under the impression that this was just Jimmy "not applying himself."

But then they went out to dinner. They were eating with a group of parents when someone mentioned their kid had failed algebra and they were disappointed. My parents said, "Really? Us too!" Soon the whole table was filled with the parents of apparent algebra dunces.

Coincidence? Not so much.

With a root cause now discovered or at least hypothesized, they went to our school and demanded to have us re-tested at the end of the summer. The school's vice-principal, who apparently didn't notice the flood of failing grades, said, "Sure. Whatever. Knock yourselves out."

And the lot of us found ourselves getting algebra tutoring over the summer and...oddly enough...*enjoying it*. Our parents had found a budding math teacher from the university in the next town—a young, funny guy. We had a great time.

We all tested at the end of the summer, got our A's and went on with our lives.

But to this day, sitting down and doing a lot of math sets me on edge. I still can't shake that sense of learned helplessness.

## WHY ELDRED CAN'T READ

Eldred, his bosses, and his co-workers have been buried under a mountain of work. And you know, it's hard to see a mountain when it's on top of you. They would not have the authority to react to the mountain even if they could.

Their company is writing code at a record pace, everyone knows the code is filled with bugs, but no one has the authority to stop working.

Lucy is not going to just sit up and say, "You know, this company has too much work. I'm going to kill my project and give my people to the other projects." Lucy works for the company, but she has been put in charge of a project. She now has people depending on her, and she is depending on her. The system that has been built governs Lucy's actions through the mechanism of politics.

Lucy's politicial construct might look something like this:

**Self Preservation** It's her job on the line.

**Why Me?** Why her and not someone else?

**This is Important** She likely believes, as do the others, that her project is the most important.

**No Power to Act** She simply lacks the authority to make that kind of proclamation.

**Not My Job** She and the other project managers are not paid to sit around second-guessing corporate decisions.

These are five great reasons (and not the only five) why Lucy the project manager is not Lucy the steward of company value.

Eldred's predicament is even worse. He cannot remove himself from any of his five projects. He knows they are all doomed. He is convinced that nothing he can do will improve the situation, because *he is also convinced of the necessity of all five projects and his role in them.* Eldred honestly believes that the projects will fail without his involvement.

Learned helplessness here means that rather than attack the root cause of the company's problems (too many projects in-flight), Eldred, his teams, and his bosses all work on treating symptoms (lateness, schedule conflicts, running over budget, apparent laziness, demotivation) as if they are the real problem. *Insidious!*

We see Eldred and his colleagues exhibiting new traits: they appear anxious, less talkative, even depressed. They begin to say things like, "Why won't people just leave me alone to do my work!?", "Why do you keep changing requirements on me!?", and the ubiquitous "Just tell me what to do!"

People are overwhelmed, overloaded, and overstimulated. All of these laments are responding to too much input with not enough clarity—a clear sign of unreasonable expectations and overwork. A lack of WIP limits results in unlimited work-in-progress.

Managers often like those laments. They feel that their existence is validated by people who need to be managed. Managers then will give direct orders to the staff. *They need clear direction!* The workers will then take that clear direction and do what they were clearly directed to.

Which seems like a good thing.

But the workers will merely do their tasks in the manner described and never ask for the context or attempt to make things better. Their expectations of what is possible deteriorate.

This means that more tasks are done without an understanding of the actual end goals. The tasks may be completed in a way that meets the description of the work, but does not actually fit into the final product. Giving knowledge workers direct commands on how to complete their work means they are no longer knowledge workers. They are simply assembling or fabricating their product. This micromanagement is great for creating highly repeatable objects like screws or push-pins, but detrimental for creating products that involve problem solving, reacting to variation, and invention.

Micromanagement creates more work at the end of a project by forcing under-informed workers to fit ill-conceived tasks into a final product—causing more delays, rework, and shoddy product. This rework, of course, is done after long, painful, and personally accusatory meetings to find out why this happened (which, of course, means who is to blame).

In addition, staff is seldom allowed to point out changes in context or easily foreseeable issues. Doing so would upset the managers who are now under a great deal of stress because they rightly feel like all the blame for schedule or cost overruns sits squarely on their shoulders. Since the decisions and their rationale were not shared, the ability to react to change is likewise not shared.

We see time and again that concentrating accountability to a handful of overburdened managers has direct negative impacts on product quality. They are truly quality bottlenecks.

Workers (who are truly workers and no longer "team members") continue to proceed until further orders come.

But…there is no one to give the orders.

That, in turn, fosters more learned helplessness.

# LIMTING WIP AS A CURE FOR LEARNED HELPLESSNESS

One day, Eldred comes to work and finds that the company has a new CEO. His name is Jayson Holt. On his first day, there is a lunch to meet and greet the new CEO. There's pizza and sodas and everyone is meeting Jayson who is smiling and affable and seems like a lot of fun. It's an all-hands, so everyone is there.

There's strange concentric rings of activity that center around Jayson.

People closest to Jayson appear very happy. Smiling and laughing.

A little ways away from Jayson, people are apprehensive.

In the outer ring people are saying things like, "This is a waste of time, I have work to do."

As Jayson Holt makes his way to the small podium everyone settles down. He declares, "My word! This company has a lot of goals and no products!"

People begin to fidget.

"Missed deadlines...quality problems...lots of good ideas...very little execution...yes..."

He looks up and smiles.

There's a pause.

"Did...any of you notice that nothing has been getting done?"

Silence.

"*...here...at...work?*"

Painful silence.

"You know...I am wondering why no one is talking. I see here that four projects are over six months delayed, yet you started a fifth. And...Project A seemed to be going really well, but then slowed down considerably. Any ideas why?"

Agonizing silence. The longer the silence, the more he smiled. He seemed to be enjoying this.

Finally Gerry couldn't take it anymore. He stands up. "We first noticed a slowdown in Project B in..." He spoke for about ten minutes providing all the reasons why Project B slowed down.

Then the other project managers spoke. All complained about numbers of meetings, coordination of shared resources, and lack of direction. Jayson listened for a long time—a painfully long time.

Then Jayson looked around the room and said, "You know what? I think it would be a capital idea if we all shelved about half this stuff for Q1 and just focused on completing a few things. You know, just to...*see what it's like to finish.*"

Stunned silence.

"For example, let's just do Projects A and B and come back to the others when we're done."

Eldred's jaw dropped. "This guy is clearly mental." He thought, "How can you finish things...by shelving things? Surely this guy is a corporate raider and layoffs start tomorrow."

Everyone, from the project managers to the rank and file, was aghast. "You can't postpone Projects C, D, and E! They're *important!*"

Eldred gives an impassioned speech for D especially. "D is the cornerstone of our entire business plan. If we never build D, we might as well not even stay in business!"

Everyone nods and mumbles their agreement with Eldred.

Jayson looks simultaneously disgusted and amused.

"Of course D is important. But...just say for a second we actually finish something. Wouldn't that be important? Wouldn't actually releasing your hard work make you, oh I don't know, *happy?*"

Blank stares greet him. Everyone knows the vision for the five projects. They all fit together. They created one big vision. Layoffs are surely imminent. C, D, and E teams are all immediately on their smartphones downloading apps from The Ladders and Monster.com.

"You don't understand," Lucy finally said. "The product roadmap has each of these projects working together."

"Do they need each other? Are they really that tightly coupled? If that's truly the case, we have one project and five project managers."

Now everyone knew there would be layoffs.

Gerry spoke after a brief silence. "Look, we get it. You want to trim a bit. We're just saying that the system is meant to be used as a cohesive whole. All five projects are separate, but in the end will all work together."

"Oh for the love of God, we're not going to lay off anyone," Jayson says. "We're going to reorg temporarily into teams focused on rapid completion of Projects A and B. Come on people, let's just *finish something.*"

No one believes him, but learned helplessness works in Jayson's favor. Everyone goes and does what they are told.

Teams are re-formed. Lots of work is painfully put on the back burner, while the front burners are turned way up.

Two new larger and dedicated teams are directed at Projects A and B. A third team—called "The Deming Team"—is specifically built to address improvements. Years of panic-driven management has resulted in tons of bad process, brittle systems, and neglected tasks. The Deming Team is there to remove the bad constraints, create healthy ones, and clean up the mess.

Eldred is steaming mad for losing Project D and the fact that it is scheduled for later in the year is of little comfort. He knows his project, Project B, will be delayed just like always. Project D will never ever be completed.

Tuesday, Eldred shows up and gets to work on Project B. At the end of the day, he is still dealing with the loss of Project D. So much so that he hardly notices, even with the coordination of the re-org, that he was very productive that day.

Wednesday, the B team gathers and talks about strategy.

Jayson shows up in the middle of the meeting.

"Hello," he says.

"What's our deadline?" Lucy asks.

"*Your* what?" he asks innocently.

"*Our* deadline."

Incredulous, he asks, "You...want me...to give you a deadline?"

She nods.

Jayson smiles. "How'd those deadlines work for you in the past?"

"What?" Lucy looks confused.

"No deadline, just get it done. You guys know how to build good software. Let's just start building, shall we?"

After Jayson closed the door, panic ran from the face of one team member to the next.

"This will drag on forever," Eldred laments.

Fifteen minutes of complaining about lack of leadership then ensues.

"You know, maybe we need to come up with our own goals for a change," Nina, the quiet and usually marginalized designer says. "Maybe we know how long it will take and Jayson doesn't. I mean, if we are right, and we've always been stopped by others from finishing stuff. Maybe now's our chance to really build something."

And they get to work creating their own plan. It doesn't come naturally. Every so often someone glances at the door, waiting for Jayson to burst in and stop them. But he doesn't. By the end of the day, they almost believe it's possible.

It feels like they've planned their own prison-break.

# CHAPTER 8
# AWARENESS

▶ **... self-discipline, that's important. Self-discipline with awareness of consequences. ~The Dalai Lama**

When we become self-aware, we shed learned helplessness. The inability to act is replaced not only by the ability to act, but something more—*the desire to act.*

Tonianne and I have seen this pattern repeatedly. We encounter teams made up of good, thoughtful people that gave up trying to help their companies in any way. They tried. Over and over they tried to improve processes, to suggest ways to save money, to alter systems so they could complete their work with higher quality. But their ideas were always shot down, often in unbelievably condescending ways.

Indifferent or hostile management creates a corporate culture of failure acceptance. This culture is so pervasive that people stop looking at problems as things to be solved and instead look at them as further evidence of how "wrong" the company is being run. Resigned, they say, "Improvement is impossible here. There's no way my boss will let me change anything."

From the management side, there is frustration as well. They say, "Why won't our people step up to the plate? Now is when we really need them!"

It's tempting at this point to write off both the workers and management. It is tempting to think that the people are lost and that the bureaucracy will take years to turn around. Indeed, there is prevailing wisdom in management consulting that it takes years to change a corporate culture.

What we've seen is quite the opposite. People that have been in a low-trust, punitive environment where action is shunned do develop learned helplessness and they do shut down, but they also create pent-up demand for change. They may have learned that they can't help now, but they're *still there* and so is their desire to help.

Eldred is still with the company, even though he was beaten down by years of being torn between multiple projects. Eldred is still there even though Eldred's friends have all told him repeatedly to get another job because this one was running him ragged.

For years, Eldred has had to marshal his self-discipline simply to avoid going insane by being pulled in so many directions. The structure of the company limited his ability to have the self-discipline of good product development and completion. Eldred never had to be aware of consequences because, other than internal political ones, he was both sheltered and ignored.

Now Eldred is a little scared. He recognizes that Team B is on the hook for completing a product—an actual product. Released to real buyers. Not only that, he recognizes that Jayson Holt isn't going to tell him or his project manager what to do. He is aware that now he won't be able to blame the system for project failure: now success or failure rests with him and his team.

On the other hand, out of the five projects in flight, Jayson unilaterally picked Projects A and B. While the teams have been given unprecedented leeway to create good software, none of this new frightening yet intoxicating freedom could have happened without Jayson starting the ball rolling.

Perhaps Jayson is trying to balance power in the company as opposed to concentrating it or abdicating it?

Eldred is also aware that no one got laid off. There was so much work not being done that the staffing still seems insufficient even for just these two projects. *How is that possible? How could all these people be fully employed after a 60% reduction in products in progress?*

Eldred is becoming aware.

Looking out his window, he puzzles it out. "We were *so busy*. We were so busy, in fact, that we were constantly negotiating how to get things done. Meetings for planning, resource allocation...does that mean most of our work was task switching? Most of our work was us managing how we managed?

"Now we're working faster. I can see it. We might even be able to get out two products in two months. Then we have three more ready to go with a long ignored wish list behind that. And…maybe now we can start responding to customer complaints faster. Or get rid of some of the buggy code."

Even with this new organization, there's still a lot of new work to be done and a lot of work to fix the quality problems in products released before the change in leadership.

Lucy stops by Eldred's cube. She wags a piece of paper in his face and says, "I just ran the numbers."

"Yes?"

"We thought this two project thing would slow us down. But it seems like by doing less, we're actually working a lot faster. At this rate, by this time next year all five projects will be released." She looks simultaneously shocked and giddy. Embarrassed, even.

Eldred nods. "I thought that was going to mean layoffs, but, when I take a look around, there's a lot of work to be done…even with fewer projects in flight."

He wonders if getting a small group together to focus and quickly work on specific features for the project would improve delivery time and increase communication. That just might work! He laughs to himself, recognizing that getting together and focusing is just another way of focusing on less things and completing the work.

Eldred sees that he could suggest short-term working groups to get features out faster. That would improve time-to-market and maybe free up staff to focus on quality issues. These "strike teams" might work. He's always wanted to try this, but never could because even he couldn't commit to it. It's an experiment, but it just might work.

Eldred just did something logical—he came up with a simple idea to get more work done. He's going to try his idea. If it works, he saves the company money and time. The cost for this experiment is next to nothing.

In the Lean management world, this is called "Kaizen," a small improvement that yields beneficial results. Overloaded Eldred was far too distracted to have time to improve his working conditions or the company's processes. Focused Eldred does this as a matter of course.

Imagine if your entire workforce was constantly and automatically improving your company because they were simultaneously improving theirs.

## ERRORS OF TITANIC PROPORTIONS

"What's up?" Jayson walks into the meeting room. The functional clutter of sticky notes, paper, white boards covered with writing makes him smile.

Lucy is furiously writing on sticky notes. She is in the in the moment. Without looking up, she uncharacteristically skips all deference and pleasantries, "We have some ideas. Sit down."

"This is awesome," Jayson says to himself and starts scanning the room—it is covered in information.

"We've been reworking Project B. We're still headed in the same direction, pretty much, but we have some changes we'd like to make."

Jayson points at the stickies...there must be 250 of them.

Lucy continues, "We want to write a change document and talk about these...um...some new features, killing others," she sighs. "There's a lot here."

Jayson says, "You're about to discuss all of those stickies aren't you?"

"Yes, we need executive buy-in," she says.

"I don't have time right now for that much buy-in," Jayson says, "I don't mind going shopping, but you've got an entire Costco here for me to buy-in on."

"Yes, we need executive buy-in." She says again.

"How many of those are actually below the waterline?"

"What?"

Jayson gets up and walks to a flip chart.

He starts to draw. "Here we have our ship of state. You

 guys are making decisions along the way. You'll run experiments. Any experiment might fail and sink the ship, right?'

"Yes, that's why we want your buy-in." Says an increasingly annoyed Lucy.

"And you think this because I know more than you about the product? Or maybe because I'm a better developer than you are? Or maybe I'm clairvoyant?"

She smirks

"GOOD! Smirking is good! Okay, so seriously, you have about a million stickies there. You don't want to explain them all to me. I don't want you to either."

"But we need buy-in," Lucy reiterates.

"Define buy-in," Jayson responds. Their volley continues.

There's a pause. "Um...agreement?"

"You got it! I agree. How's that?"

"But you don't know what they are."

"Nope."

Silence.

Jayson probes, *"Does that...scare you?"* He makes horror movie movements with his arms.

"Yes."

"Do *all those stickies* scare you?"

"Um...uh...no?" she says tentatively.

"But some do."

"Yes..."

Jayson turns back to his ship drawing and says, "Look, a lot of these changes you make might go wrong and poke holes in our ship. Some of them are up 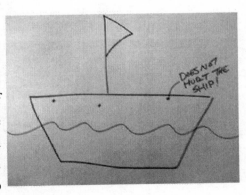 here." He draws some dots at the top of the ship. "See? These are the stickies you don't care about."

"Because, even if they go wrong, they don't really hurt the ship...we won't sink."

"BINGO! That's called learning! We want to learn, but we don't want to go crazy, we still want to use good judgment. Now these," Jayson draws some dots well below the waterline.

"These scare the crap out of you! They'll sink the ship! I'll bet you guys can tell me which stickies those are."

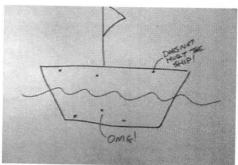

"Yes, in fact I already have some of them over here…"

"Okay, now we have the ones in this gray area…" He dots a few a little above, at, and a little below the waterline. "These… are a little tricky."

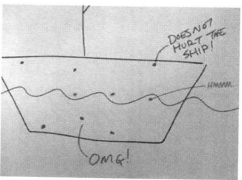

Lucy and the team nod. Eldred tries not to laugh. The old CEO and this guy couldn't be more different.

"Here's what I want you to do. I want you to put these stickies on the wall. The top of the wall is the top of the ship, the bottom of the wall is the bottom of the ship. This is not just for Lucy, it's for all three of you. And no one speaks. So, without talking I want you guys to put those stickies where they'd be relative to the water line. I'm going to get myself something from the kitchen. When I come back in about five minutes, I expect you'll be done or at least pretty close to it."

Jayson stands up and walks out of the room.

"Wait! On the wall...where's the water line?" Lucy yells after him.

"I don't care!" Jayson's words echo in the hall.

Crazy Larry, Eldred, and Lucy stare at each other.

"Dude's the freaking Willy Wonka of management," Crazy Larry says.

They start to put stickies on the wall. Lucy puts something high up. Eldred takes the sticky and moves it down lower.

"You can't do that!" She cries out.

Eldred puts his finger to his lips while Crazy Larry wags a disapproving finger at her.

The three laugh and sort the stickies. As a group, they're starting to click. It's understood that if someone moves a sticky down, it stays down.

When Jayson returns, he takes a look at the wall. He ponders the stickies. He reaches up and moves two more down below the water line.

Lucy opens her mouth to say something like, "See, I knew we needed buy-in," but now she sees something else. In a few short minutes everyone saw what the product roadmap was. Everyone picked what needed to be discussed and what did not.

Jayson and the team discuss what needs to be discussed. They do not discuss low risk changes unless they become relevant. These tasks become known as "safe-to-fail" tasks. Lucy notes that Jayson rarely questions any decision made by the team, but instead focuses on the impacts. The team already knows which tasks are the risky ones and are therefore more interested in discussing them or seeking Jayson's opinion.

At one point she asks, "You're really not interested in those up there, are you?"

"Nope."

"What if we're wrong?"

"Then we're wrong. It happens every day. But look, you guys are professionals. This is your product as much as anyone's. If I control everything, then it isn't your product anymore. It becomes mine and you become the monkeys that code for me. That's why we limited our WIP, you know?

"We limited WIP to get focus—so you guys could make these decisions. So you'd really know the waterline. So we could finish something and, when we were done, everyone would know what it was and why we did it. So you guys didn't have to get buy-in for simple, logical, and professional decisions. We did it because, when people are overworked, they can't trust their own work, let alone their colleagues'.

"My hope is not to move any stickies. I moved those two because they impact partnering initiatives that we have in the company. But, strange as it may sound, my CEO risk assessment is different than your risk assessment as engineers. If you are overloaded with work to the point that you can't assess risk, I am in turn overloaded with even more risk to assess. And I won't assess engineering risk very well. Today, you guys told me a lot about our engineering risk and I got to share with you some business risk. That's only going to help us in the long run."

# AWARENESS: ELDRED'S UNEXPECTED BONUS

Limiting WIP for Eldred and Team B has allowed everyone to avoid distraction and focus on understanding their product. They have been able to "slow down" and notice where waste can be prevented and they can complete higher quality work with less effort. This leaves previously wasted effort to be reinvested in other areas of the business.

Limiting context switching has raised the **productivity** of the group. An increasingly coherent product narrative is emerging: they know what they are building and why. An increase in project coherence has made them much more **effective**. They are making small but meaningful changes in process creating an **efficient** operation. They can see inefficiencies, they have more time to talk to customers, and they have a shared understanding of the product itself.

Awareness required one other element: agency. Eldred and his team needed to be able to act on the improvement opportunities they recognized. Without agency, the teams would have to ask permission to make even slight process changes. That permission would require memos, meetings, justification, and delay—which would quickly destroy any value the process improvement might have had.

# CHAPTER 9
# COMMUNICATION

"Good morning, Eldred."

"Good morning, Jayson."

Before Jayson Holt came on board, there was zero contact with the CEO, except maybe a perfunctory exchange of pleasantries at the annual holiday party. The CEO might as well have been a movie star—someone you recognized but didn't dare approach. He certainly wasn't someone who would take the time to know your name.

Jayson, on the other hand, quickly became a regular at stand-up meetings. He'd participate, but not dictate. At first Eldred thought he was there to keep his eye on the teams, but this was more than oversight. It was like this guy was actually *interested*.

What was surprising was everyone in the company now seemed more interested in operations, in development, in...*everything*. Team A members were stopping by for stand-ups, coming to Team B demos, and regularly checking out project boards.

Now, Eldred's team was suspiciously close to delivering. Actually shipping product to customers.

One afternoon, Jayson comes into Team B's space and looks up at the kanban. Without having to ask, he sees what's in progress, what's complete, and what is almost done.

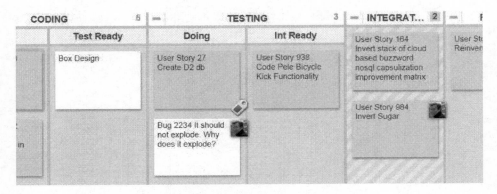

"That looks good!" he says to Eldred.

There was no briefing. There was no status meeting. He can see that work is flowing. That two tasks are completed and three more are in acceptance testing. Soon they'll be ready as well. No tickets are marked as blocked or as a problem.

The team is within their WIP limits—3 out of 5 for CODING, 3 for TESTING, 2 for INTEGRATION.

Eldred says with a smile, "If the *box design* is out of development today, the rest is easy. We have a working session on that today, right? I think we'll knock it out."

After years of shoddy or no releases, they are releasing something after a matter of months—and that feels good. It feels like work was supposed to feel. It feels like progress.

From the leadership side of things, Jayson knows his company is going to release. Lucy knows her team is on schedule. The company's board of directors can see the teams' kanban boards, they see the flow, they've even seen the demos. But they are removed from the action. They are, at this point at least, cautiously optimistic.

## COMMUNICATION AND LIMITING WIP

The WIP limits for the team enable flow of work, they also limit the work being undertaken to a reasonable level. On Team B's board, Jayson is able to quickly grasp what is going on. So can the members of Team B, so can members of Team A. Everyone can see the simple story that is this project.

That instant information transfer from the kanban to anyone who views it means that no one on the team had to tell Jayson their status. Since nothing is blocked or shows a status of pain, there is no need to talk about status in depth. We don't need to discuss things that are obvious or going well.

Much of our time in status meetings is spent discussing normal events—people doing what they should in a way that they should. Discussing these in meetings sends two messages to knowledge workers: (1.) we want to check on everything you are doing and (2.) we will give final approval of everything you are doing. This is wasted energy, wasted time, wasted money, wasted potential, and leads to learned helplessness.

In his conversation with Jayson, Eldred mentioned one feature in particular, the box design, because it was relevant and he was excited about it.

Time-consuming communication can now be reserved for things people actually need to talk about or for working sessions.

In addition, the board is always visible. If something becomes blocked or in danger, the board communicates that, too. And it communicates that immediately and dispassionately.[1]

Without limiting WIP, the board's conversation becomes much less compelling. Having a simple "task board" with no WIP limits only communicates the existence of work. We never know if people are overburdened. We will likely have an incomprehensible number of tickets on the board. Tickets will enter the board and languish for long periods of time. When questioned, people will say, "Yeah, I'm just not working on that right now" and will continue to say that as the board fills with the trivial and the catastrophic until stickies overlap and severity is irrelevant.

---

1        For much more detail on how, specifically, the board does this, see Tonianne DeMaria Barry, MemeMachine II, Why Kanban Works, Seattle, Modus Cooperandi Press, 2014.

# CHAPTER 10
## LEARNING

In "Chapter 5: Creating an Economy," we discussed four elements we need to understand in order to build our economy. The third was that knowledge work involves learning. Learning is a deep subject—we might think of it as simply taking in, synthesizing, and storing new information—but it is much more. Our history impacts our present by providing us with a "world-view" that guides much of what we see.

In *Why Kanban Works*, we discuss metacognition and double loop learning. Metacognition is learning about learning. Double loop learning is, in short, studying how you study. These two concepts combine with the awareness brought on by limiting our WIP to create a system of perpetual experimentation, dynamic focus, and learning.

As knowledge workers, we need to learn. If we do not learn, our products will never improve. If new products from knowledge workers are not improvements, the market will have no need for them. If the market is buying innovation, we have an innovation economy. In an innovation economy, improvement is more important than productivity.

But how do knowledge workers learn? They learn by doing, by observing, by experimenting, through direction, and by adjusting.

**Doing** We learn best through direct experience. If I have a four hour PowerPoint presentation about how to play Super Mario Brothers, you will understand that my little pixelated guy can jump on turtles or blocks, that sometimes he's big and sometimes he's small, and that you can collect coins. But you would learn much more simply playing the game. Knowledge workers learn a considerable amount just by working on a project. It is through doing we come to fully understand our work.

**Observing** There is much in the average project to observe. Some tasks are easy, others more difficult. Sometimes tasks we are expecting to be simple and straightforward wind up being complex and confounding. There are personal conflicts. There are political struggles. The market for our product changes every day. Our competition is releasing their own versions of our product with different features and design sensibilities. We can either observe these trends or ignore them. Through interested observation, we become aware. With awareness, we can act thoughtfully.

**Experimenting** In doing and observing we note discrepancies between the way things are and way they could potentially could be. We build hypotheses about how to mitigate these discrepancies. We experiment to see if our hypotheses are correct. If they are not, then we learn and try again. If they are, we learn, we are happy, and move on to the next thing to improve. We are careful to try to disprove our hypotheses, not just to prove them. We build on our previous work as well, extending previous successes and learning from failures.

**Direction** Here our learning is directed. We know what we are looking for. We have directed, purposeful learning. We seek out aticles, books, or videos that can quickly help us respond to problems and test hypotheses. When we are aware, we have a better idea of where the gaps in our knowledge are. What would otherwise be unknown unknowns become known unknowns. We can engage in directed learning because we know there is a need for the information, rather than just because of current management fads or because someone orders us to. In this case, reading or classes augment our observations and experiments. At this point, short lectures (even PowerPoints) can be very helpful in rapid, focused learning.

**Adjusting** Learning is humbling. It makes us reassess our current processes and replace them with others. Sometimes learning comes with huge adjustments called epiphanies. Sometimes adjustments are simply minor.

# PLAN DO [CHECK / STUDY /REFLECT] ACT

▶ **Awards become corroded, friends gather no dust. ~Jesse Owens**

Before Jayson Holt began with the company, one person on each of Eldred's teams had to generate weekly reports showing project health. On-time performance, productivity, quality, defects corrected, staff utilization, and more—all with corresponding numbers, charts, and graphs—were key performance indicators (KPIs). Each KPI had a target value.

Every week, reports were submitted to upper management and numbers that fell below their targets would be discussed. In good times, these reports slowed work and frustrated staff. In times of trouble, discussions were inquisitions—using the numbers to justify blame (which they called "accountability").

These reports rarely made people happy or resulted in anything actionable; no actual learning occurred.

The reports merely showed what had happened, with no context. To prove this, all one had to do was ask, "How often do our metrics help us attain our goals?" *If you are gathering metrics and still failing...it's a pretty good bet the metrics are not helping you solve your problems.*

Business in this situation quickly finds itself paying more attention to metrics than to actual success. To help replace metrics-fetishism with useful contextual learning, W. Edwards Deming gave us the Plan, Do, Check, Act (PDCA) cycle. The PDCA cycle was based on the premise that we can't learn without understanding what we are learning, and we can't understand without testing. So, we plan what we'd like to see, we do it for a short time, then we check the results, and then that leads to *informed* action.

Usually, people just skip the first three and go straight to "Act."

Deming later revised this cycle to Plan, Do, Study, Act (PDSA). We may, in turn, give that a personal twist of Plan, Do, Reflect, Act (PDRA).

Why is that third part so difficult? Why study, why reflect, why not check? It all rests on how we approach our work.

Deming started with "Check," but over time he realized the word "Check" was a loaded one. Check implied measurement—with heavy metrics and KPIs, it meant statistical process control. And that was precisely what he was trying to avoid.

Deming had 14 core points for approaching work in a rational way, the 11th of which took this head-on:[1]

> 11. a. Eliminate work standards (quotas) on the factory floor. Substitute with leadership.
> b. Eliminate management by objective.
> Eliminate management by numbers and numerical goals. Instead substitute with leadership.

For Deming, it was clear that any metric we chose told a story, but no complete story is told by one variable. Here is a story with one variable: *Jesse Owens ran very fast*. Clearly this statement grossly understates the Olympian's role in history. To get a complete picture of what Jesse Owens

---

W. Edwards Deming, *Our of the Crisis*, MIT Press, Cambridge, 1982

meant you actually have to understand what it meant to be Jesse Owens. We need context. We need understanding.

We often run extremely large, complex businesses on unbelievably limited and misleading information. Unfortunately, the "Check" in PDCA has been used to justify all sorts of myopic data-gathering efforts in business. People often search for the "key metric" that could judge all performance and risk. But that's not what Deming meant.

Later in life, Deming replaced "Check" with "Study." He didn't want you to *measure* what you were doing, he wanted you to actually *understand* it. Sometimes this involves measuring, but more often it involves observing and appreciating.

We at Modus say "Reflect" to punctuate that the work we are doing requires careful thought—not automated numbers—to gain understanding. When a series of events happens, we need to take some time and think.

So, Eldred and his colleagues used to gather numbers to present each week. They would then discuss numbers that showed the results of what had happened in their recent past. Each week, they would respond posthumously to problems that became apparently apparent.

*Apparently apparent?*

Yes, because often they were discussing normal fluctuations in numbers—some weeks are good, some weeks not so good. It was foolish to penalize not so good weeks, when statistically those were normal fluctuations in the numbers. People were gathering the numbers, they knew what they were supposed to mean, but not what they *actually meant.*

Each number had a target. Management had goals and wanted to achieve these goals. When they didn't, that was sad. When they did, that was wonderful! But in the end, the failures and the successes didn't lead to products being released, they didn't lead to improvement, and they didn't even lead to understanding. They led to nervously or pathologically watching numbers.

Who won in that scenario? Teams with goals substantially lower than their capabilities. Teams who got lucky and had a sustained period of performance. Teams that sucked less than their counterparts. All this is a way of saying, people won when they didn't get into trouble—which is not a recipe for innovation or performance.

When Jayson took over leadership of the company, demand for those reports remained. Staff was still burdened by creating the reports, but they too had history with them. They felt good when the numbers were good and felt bad when they were not. They were constantly doing things to improve those numbers.

The group was suffering a combination of:

- **Loss Aversion (Sunk Cost Fallacy)** The tendency for people to want to continue doing something they've started, simply because they've already invested their time and energy in it;

WHY LIMIT WIP

- **Status Quo Bias** The tendency to want to keep doing what is familiar; and

- **Information Bias** The tendency to seek more information, even when that information is not helpful.

Most business floats in this cognitive bias soup. Metrics are seen as scientific (they are not) simply because they are numbers we can gather. But metrics gathered without cause are seldom helpful. As we gather them, we get caught up in the false narrative that these metrics comprise. Sometimes we "beat" the metrics, sometimes they "beat" us. We always want to come back for another round.

Since we believe these numbers are scientific, we believe they are useful. We search for new ways to use these numbers, even though they haven't helped us in the past. But Information Bias makes us want the information, which we've sunk time into gathering and...*can you see the system building here?*

~

In his first Monday morning meeting, Jayson Holt looked at the stack of reports and asked, "What do these mean?"

Response was immediate. "Productivity is up 3%, defects are down .5%, we were able to deliver half our features in the last release."

"What does it mean that productivity is up 3%?"

"Um…that we are doing 3% more work than last week."

"How does that change how you do your work?"

"Well, we know we're getting better."

"At what?"

*Pause*

Jayson set the paper on the table and said, "What if we never do these again?"

"We won't know how we are doing."

"How about we measure success not by these numbers but by delivering products? Gary, how much time do you spend doing the numbers for your team?"

Gary thinks for a moment and says, "Well, heads-down time…about 4 hours."

"And heads-up time?"

He turns an interesting shade of red, "I'm not sure…"

Folding his hands, Jayson says, "I'll make you a deal. Let's not do these reports for three weeks. If we miss them, we can go back to them."

"Jayson," Eldred says, "how will you know what we're doing? How will you know we're on the right track?"

"We'll pay attention to you and the product, not these charts and graphs. The kanban tells me all I need to know."

"But, these are how we know how we're doing. Without them we're...blind."

"Please show me the number...any number...that you can make a decision with right now. Show me any number that causes direct action today. For that matter, show me a number that has caused you to take direct action in the last six months."

The ensuing conversation was painful. The teams showed Jayson times when numbers were good, but could never come up with a direct cause. They showed times when numbers were bad and gave weak responses like, "We worked really hard to fix that." Specifics were embarrassingly unavailable.

Since Jayson was CEO, he had the final say. The numbers-gathering stopped. Project managers felt an immediate loss. Much of their week was tied up making sure the reports were up-to-date. Some of them kept doing it surreptitiously. But they couldn't get the staff to supply numbers, so they gradually stopped asking.

Staff that previously spent days preparing reports were now free to work on projects. Team productivity and effectiveness rose immediately; strangely enough they had more time to work. The visualizations and WIP-limiting of the kanban showed events as they happened.

Jayson was regularly walking the halls, sitting in on design meetings, and actively participating.

When metrics fluctuated, which they do naturally, they ceased to be after-the-fact emergencies and blame games. Instead these observations became real-time items to study and, only when necessary, correct. Personally, Eldred found he was happy getting rid of the stress-filled Monday morning meetings. Gary soon realized the weight of report preparation.

As the weeks passed, the team found they missed only two metrics out of the pages they had previously gathered. These were now actionable numbers. A team set to work automating those, so the team and management could get real-time and historic information without burdening staff. More unnecessary work-in-progress eliminated to free up energy for the real work.

## LIMITING WIP AND LEARNING: THE ONSET OF AGENCY

Limiting WIP gives us the flow and coherence we've discussed throughout this MemeMachine. It is not a panacea, but it is an extremely powerful tool. **Consider WIP limiting a pre-requisite more than a cure-all.** If you (or your team or company) are not limiting work-in-progress, then you are likely distracted, overburdened, and unlikely to innovate.

Limiting WIP is not going to instantly and magically create a flawless workforce. Anyone making claims that an out-of-the-box process will instantly result in hyper-productivity is a snake oil salesman. Even after driver's ed class, we still have to steer the car.

What limiting WIP will do, however, is promote the growth of agency. When Eldred began to see himself setting policy by starting working groups, when he became comfortable with the thought of completion, he was gaining agency.

The trick here was that none of the project managers could truly provide Eldred agency. They also didn't have the authority. Only Jayson Holt could truly give the people in the company the ability to act on their ideas. He had to set policies and expectations that would both support that decision making and not hinder it.

Limiting work-in-progress was vital in this effort because overloaded people simply can't develop the understanding necessary to affect thoughtful change. To be sure, overloaded people can come up with endless suggestions for change, but it's unlikely those suggestions will be thoughtful. They are more likely to be reactive to overload. Overloaded people work on their work (the tasks in front of them), they don't work on *the way they work* (improving the product and the company).

## WHAT WOULD HAPPEN IF JAYSON WAS EVIL?

In "normal" businesses, we don't have a Jayson Holt. We might even have managers that would be the anti-Jayson or the Evil Jayson. In this case, management is focused solely on getting projects out the door and will not tolerate anything that appears to delay progress. Of course, they do this while taking on too much work and stalling progress. So what would this look like?

Evil Jayson would have rejected the idea that there was too much WIP.

Evil Jayson would think the people in the company needed consensus, understanding, and action. He would reason, "If people only understood what they were supposed to do, they'd just *do it.*"

He wouldn't have limited PIP (projects-in-progress). He would have insisted that the real problem was that people needed to *understand* why **all** the projects in progress were *critical*...because *then* they could focus.

Evil Jayson would spell out the importance of each project, implementing a burning platform strategy, insisting that the company was going to collapse if all the projects didn't get done *right this very minute.* The death march to completion, taking up everyone's nights and weekends would then commence.

Evil Jayson would create many metrics and set targets for each one. He would then become legendary for his punitive tirades against any and all who didn't meet their targets. He would, however, sit smiling as people brought him fabricated reports that appeared to satisfy the goals.

Evil Jayson would think the problem is that people have the ability to focus, but they are just too lazy to do so. The best way, therefore, to get people to focus is to place them in competition with each other, providing awards for people who worked the fastest, the longest, or the hardest.

Evil Jayson would divide and conquer throughout the organization by undermining decision making by the workers, changing the definitions of the products without notice, and introducing week-long trainings for processes no one has ever heard of right before a deadline.

Evil Jayson would, as the maraschino cherry atop this sundae of pain, place posters with slogans about happiness and fairness on the walls and tell everyone that they represent the very best of what it meant to work for Evil Enterprises and that they should all adhere to these core principles.

Evil Jayson would focus on anything and everything but logically and quickly completing valuable products.

Evil Jayson…is evil.

So, don't be Evil Jayson. Limit Your WIP and set your Eldred free.

# EPILOGUE:
# NO REALLY, LIMIT WIP

Over the last eight years, in our travels globally, we have noticed a nearly universal need to limit work-in-progress. We have worked with groups as diverse as social scientists in Vietnam to consulting engineers in Toronto to software developers in Milwaukee to megabureaucratic Fortune 10 companies and government agencies.

We've repeatedly found that overloading individuals and teams destroys value, morale, and culture. Companies with dozens of simultaneous year-or-more-delayed projects are easy to find. Staff and management alike blame these delays on the knowledge workers themselves. They blame them on process. They blame them on bad middle managers. They blame them on perceived anomalies (blizzards, flu epidemics, etc).

Once, on the first day of an engagement, our client looked us in the eye and said, "I'm not sure what you can do, we don't really have the best people here."

*Um...*

Needless to say, the people were great. It was the system in which they worked that was horrendous.

This is the tip of the iceberg. We haven't even begun to discuss the psychological storm most business managers find themselves in today. In addition to the Planning Fallacy, Google terms like *"Comparison Bias,"* *"Fundamental Attribution Error,"* and *"Illusion of Control"* to start. Or you can pick up a copy of *Why Plans Fail* - our MemeMachine on Cognitive Bias. There are ample forces working against both managers and workers.

But for now...

If you are in a company with many long-overdue projects try these simple steps:

1.  Count the bosses. Who has more than 3? (Anyone who does is an Eldred).

2.  Add up the total months projects have been delayed.

3.  Add up the total months projects were expected to take.

4.  Subtract #3 from #2.

5.  After you finish crying / laughing, ask yourself, "What is the cost of this delay?" (If it's zero, your product is worthless or you are lying).

6.  Then ask, "What would happen if you put some projects on hold and focused on others?"

7.  Then ask, "What would a truly finished product look like?" "What would it feel like?"

You might be surprised that the answers are easier than your learned helplessness lets you think.

# WHY LIMIT WIP
# & SOCIAL MEDIA

The MemeMachine series has been designed to start conversations. We want you to take these ideas and build on them.

Modus Cooperandi and Modus Institute have several channels to discuss these ideas.

We would love to continue the conversation we've begun here.

If you tweet, follow and engage us we are @ourfounder and @sprezzatura. Use the hashtag #moduscoop.

On LinkedIn, discuss visualizing work and limiting WIP at: https://www.linkedin.com/groups/Personal-Kanban-3795393

And find other avenues at moduscooperandi.com

# AFTERWORD
## & ACKNOWLEDGEMENTS

This MemeMachine completes a series of sorts. MemeMachine I, *Why Plans Fail* and MemeMachine II, *Why Kanban Works,* combine to create the foundation for a paradigm of project management. This paradigm is based squarely on the teachings of Dr. W. Edwards Deming, work by neo-Lean thinkers, and the experiences of software development in the Agile era. We extend this work with recent developments in cognitive science, psychology, economics, and sociology.

In writing this MemeMachine, I drew, of course, from the inspiration that is Tonianne DeMaria Barry. I also was blessed to have Jabe Bloom, Paul Klipp, Ann Miner, Steve Holt, and Jason Montague follow along in Google Docs and give me persistent, diverse, and dogged feedback. Thank you all, your viewpoints were so different and your edits reflected that. This work would be much less than what it is without your input and support.

# ABOUT
# JIM BENSON

Jim Benson's background in psychology, urban planning, and software development have seen him
build light rail systems and neigh-
borhoods, enterprise software and
web sites and, most recently, helping create better working environ-
ments for teams of all sizes as the
CEO of Modus Cooperandi. The

common thread throughout his history has been the systems, collaboration, and methods of problem solving.

With Modus, Jim has worked with corporate, government, and not-for-profit organizations of all sizes. He
helps clients create sustainable collaborative / Lean management systems. He and his company combine Lean
principles from manufacturing, Agile methodologies
from software design, and the recent revelations in cognitive psychology, as process and tool infrastructure. The
key to making those tools work, however, is developing a
culture that supports them.

Jim is the creator of Personal Kanban, a system for visualizing and controlling knowledge work, and a pioneer in the field of Lean Management for knowledge workers. His book Personal Kanban is a global bestseller and winner of the Shingo Research and Publication Award. He is also a fellow in the Lean Systems Society and a 2012 winner of the Brickell Key Award for Excellence in Lean Thinking.

# MODUS COOPERANDI
## BOARD WALKS &
## LAUNCH READY

Modus Cooperandi is led by Jim Benson, a kanban pioneer who began using the tool in 2005 at his software company Gray Hill Solutions. Since then, Jim has worked with world governments, Fortune 10 companies, startups and everything in between.

He has co-written *Personal Kanban: Mapping Work | Navigating Life* with Tonianne DeMaria Barry. Together, they have taken kanban from software into accounting, law, international development, consulting engineering, and more.

While the elements in this book can be immediately applied to your organization, for a deeper dive you can retain Modus to train or consult with your teams. We help organizations limit work-in-progress, build flow-based systems, understand the work currently in flight, and improve processes in real-time.

# DEDICATED KAIZEN CAMP ™

This is a one- or two-day event of 12 to 100 people. A Kaizen Camp is a day of facilitated internal discussions where people in an organization explore how they work, and ways to improve how they work. Kaizen Camp attendees have included Microsoft, the Gates Foundation, Siemens, Amazon, Telstra, BT, Boeing, and more. The goal of an internal Kaizen Camp is both to surface issues impeding the organization and begin efforts to solve them. Participants leave Kaizen Camps knowing that their work and their working environment will improve, which makes them happier, more attentive, and more likely to implement the changes discussed.

# LEAN COACHING / BOARD WALKS

This is a half-day or a full day of visits to teams within an organization. We discuss how they currently work, what is impeding their work, and any issues that impact either team health or personal happiness. We then use Lean techniques to help the team understand, examine, and solve these issues. If the teams already have a kanban or Personal Kanban, we discuss the boards in detail, making sure they are optimized to their specific needs.

# TRAINING AND CLASSES

We offer half day or full day classes in the following topics. Half day classes tend to be mostly lecture, while full day classes are more participatory:

## Kanban and Personal Kanban

This training gives teams an immediately implementable tool set to visualize their work, understand their capacity, and increase quality. This is not the implementation a new process, but a way to visualize and improve what a team is already doing. Using a kanban can help a team optimize their processes to their client, their product, and their culture.

## Root Cause Analysis

This class provides teams with an immediately implementable methodology to explore issues and solve them rationally. The class discusses why we want to surface root causes, why we often find the wrong ones, and how to increase the potential for both finding the right causes and dealing with them effectively. The Modus RCA methodology begins by creating a large set of potential issues surrounding the problem, systematically analyzing those issues, finding real candidate root causes, and running real experiments to find the right ones.

## Attentive Management

This course is for managers who want to understand the psychology of work, how to pay attention to multiple projects, how to calm their personal workload, when to delegate, smart hiring, the use of kanban to communicate goals, and the use of kanban to plan and forecast better. This is a class tailored for managers who find themselves overwhelmed with work.

# LAUNCH READY

Launch Ready is a one to three week intensive session to launch a team or an organization into production. Think of this as the zero-to-sixty event. We will:

- Train staff on Lean applications including Personal Kanban, A3, Five Whys, Kaizen, and Customer Value.

- Map out initial value streams

- Help teams and the organization understand the initial feature set

- Help teams and the organization understand how information and decision making currently flows

- Help teams build their initial boards

- Help teams build initial policies for delivery

- Launch

We have worked throughout the US, Europe, and Asia – travel is not a problem as long as the work is interesting.

# CONTACT

Modus is reachable at moduscooperandi.com Or you can reach Jim Benson personally at:

jim@moduscooperandi.com

# MODUS COOPERANDI PRESS
## GROUNDBREAKING WORKS IN CONTINUOUS IMPROVEMENT

## PERSONAL KANBAN

### By Jim Benson and Tonianne DeMaria Barry

Winner of the 2013 Shingo Research and Publication Award.

Machines need to be productive. People need to be effective. Productivity books focus on doing more, Jim and Tonianne want you to focus on doing better. Personal Kanban is about choosing the right work at the right time. Recognizing why we do the things we do. Understanding the impact of our actions. Creating value — not just product. For ourselves, our families, our friends, our co-workers. For our legacy. Personal Kanban takes the same Lean principles from manufacturing that led the Japanese auto industry to become a global leader in quality, and applies them to individual and team work. Personal Kanban asks only that we visualize our work and limit our work-in-progress. Visualizing work allows us to transform our conceptual and threatening workload into an actionable, context-sensitive flow. Limiting our work-in-progress helps us complete what we start and understand the value of our choices. Combined, these two simple acts encourage us to improve the way we work and the way we make choices to balance our personal, professional, and social lives. Neither a prescription nor a plan, Personal Kanban provides a light, actionable, achievable framework for understanding our work and its context. This book describes why students, parents, business leaders, major corporations, and world governments all see immediate results with Personal Kanban.

# BEYOND AGILE

## By Maritza van den Heuvel, Joanne Ho and Jim Benson

Beyond Agile provides a broad but strong foundation for agile practices, but it doesn't stop there. After grounding us in solid theory, Beyond Agile takes us beyond the typical business book, diving deep into the ongoing practices of real teams doing real work. The stories bust many myths about agile and shares the human stories of real people and their struggles, trials and triumphs. Each story makes the complex and evolving topic of agile in the workplace engagingly clear and simple. *Beyond Agile is a great, foundational and inspiring book.* ~ Dave Gray, Author of Gamestorming and The Connected Company Software development is knowledge work. Knowledge work is always an evolving art. Beyond Agile examines 10 companies, mostly in the tech world, but also in innovative automotive and business consulting, that have actively evolved their processes. Using tools from Lean, Agile and other schools of management thought, these companies have actively engaged in continuous improvement. These stories are stories of success, failure, and success again. These are real stories of real businesses creating real products. No story is devoid of mis-steps. No magic bullets, other than understanding, are provided. Collecting stories from several continents and countries, these case studies cover the global evolution of an entire industry. This book is a must-read for anyone involved with knowledge workers, software developers and IT shops that seem unmanageable.

# SCRUMBAN

## By Corey Ladas

Corey Ladas' groundbreaking paper "ScrumBan" has captured the imagination of the software development world. Scrum and agile methodologies have helped software development teams organize and become more efficient. Lean methods like kanban can extend these benefits. Kanban also provides a powerful mechanism to identify process improvement opportunities. This book covers some of the metrics and day-to-day management techniques that make continuous improvement an achievable outcome in the real world. ScrumBan the book provides a series of essays that give practitioners the background needed to create more robust practices combining the best of agile and lean.

# WHY PLANS FAIL

## By Jim Benson

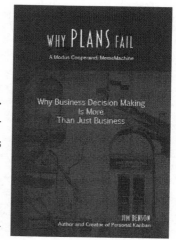

Business runs on decisions. Recently, we've discovered that people aren't the great decision makers we thought they were.

Business relies on estimates, plans, and projections - and we all know how accurate they tend to be. Careers are made, careers are broken based on accurate estimation and planning.

But what if the successes and failures of these projects were not based on the prowess of those making the plans? What if success or failure were more often the result of a more complex set of events?

Why Plans Fail directly addresses our ability of to plan, to forecast, and to make decisions.

This short work is the first in the Modus Cooperandi MemeMachine series - which looks specifically at underlying issues that directly impact the success of teams, companies, and individuals. The MemeMachine series is meant to start conversations and advance discussion.

# WHITE PAPER 1: KANBAN: DIVERSITY AND OPTIMIZATION OF KNOWLEDGE WORKING TEAMS

## By Jim Benson

KINDLE ONLY

Late in 2012, we conducted a Board Walk (a site visit where we meet with teams using Kanban or Personal Kanban and help them optimize the board and the team itself) at a client in the United States. There were 15 individual teams, each of which had its own individually designed boards. Each board had a unique value stream, work item types, policies, and methods for judging completeness and quality.

Both management and the teams were frustrated because they hadn't yet found a board design that worked for the entire company. They were looking for standardization.

However, each of these boards were, in some way, optimized for each individual team. Each team had its own context and these boards related specifically to that context. Each team was also actively improving their boards on a regular basis – meaning that optimization was continuing.

This white paper contrasts many of these boards, showing the differences in design of each board and the ramifications of those variations.

# WHITE PAPER 2: THE CLIENT MANAGEMENT A3

## By Jim Benson

KINDLE ONLY

We examine a mashup between the Lean A3 decision making and experimentation tool and the Persona tool from software development. The blend of these two techniques provides insights both into controlled business process experimentation and the recognition of the impacts of individuals in our processes.w

Made in the USA
Middletown, DE
18 April 2016